AVOIDING COSTLY HIRING MISTAKES

Mario S. Pecoraro

Table of Contents

Introduction 1
    Investigation and Human Resources 2
    The Bottom Line 3

Chapter One: The Definition of Risk in the Employment World 5
    The Risk of Employment 5
        The Cost of a Bad Hire 6
    Other Employment Scenarios 7
        Gig Workers 7
        Subcontractors 9
        How Do We Manage This in the Organization? 10
    Overall Company-Wide Risks 10
        1. Physical/Workplace Risks 10
        2. Cyber Risks 11
        3. Social Risks 11
    What Does a Breach Cost Your Organization? 12

Chapter Two: Talent & Hiring Process 15
    Recruitment and Selection 15
    The Interview Process 16
        Determining Culture/Personality Fit 17
        Determining Skills 18
        Determining Physical Health 18
        Determining Other Elements 18
    The Finalists 19
    Background Investigation Time 19
    Is This Going Too Far? 22
    If They're Lying About X, What Else Are They Lying About? .. 24

Not All Background Checks Are Created Equal 24
    1. Private Sector Background Checks 25
    2. Public Sector Background Checks 26

How Things Used to Be 27

How Things Are Now 28
    1. Application 28
    2. Release Form 28
    3. Disclosure 29
    4. Other Documents 29
    5. International Issues 29
    6. Limitations 29

A Contingent Offer? 30

The Results are In: To Hire or Not to Hire? 31
    Hiring 31
    Not Hiring 31

Mitigating Hiring Risks 32

Chapter Three: Subcontractors, Gig Workers, and More 35

Other Employment Scenarios 35

The Unique Challenges of Non-Traditional Workers 36

Gig Workers, Subcontractors, and Contractors, Oh My! 37

Risk Factor Issues 38
    Issues Surrounding Large Contractors 39
    Issues Surrounding Gig Workers 40

What Should You Do? 41
    1. Establish Guidelines 41
    2. Consider the Legal Guidelines 42
    3. Establish a Contract/Agreement 42
    4. Ensure Your Status 43

Chapter Four: Post-Employment Screening and Due Diligence ... 45

Routine Post-Employment Screening 45
    Infinity Screening 45
    Incident-Based Screening 47
    Injury-Based Screening 48

Why Is This So Important? 48
    As Part of Your Risk-Mitigation Strategy 48
    Because of Negligent Retention Liability 49

Processes and Considerations for Post-Employment Screening .. 50

What About Subcontractors and Gig Workers? 52

Chapter Five: Legal Implications and Concerns 53

The Basics 53

What Does the FCRA Require? 54
    1. Time Frame 54
    2. Non-Compliance 55
    3. Additional Requirements 56
    4. Procedural Requirements of the FCRA 56
    5. State Requirements 57

What About the EEOC? 58

And the FTC? 59

Other Legal Trends 60
    1. Ban the Box 60
    2. Salary History 61
    3. Use of Credit Reports 61
    4. Drug Testing and Marijuana 62

Chapter Six: Hiring-Specific Policies and Procedures 65

The Importance of Policies and Procedures 65

Hiring-Specific Concerns 66

Candidate-Selection Policy Concerns 67

Other Procedures, Policies, and Best Practices 70
    1. Onboarding 70
    2. Retention and Engagement 71
    3. Leave 71
    4. Post-Hire Investigations 71

A Successful Hire 72

Chapter Seven: Best Practices: Employees 73

- Policies and Procedures 73
    - Onboarding 73
    - Your Employee Handbook 75
    - Career Planning 75
    - Culture, Core Values, and Mission 76
    - Company Policies and Disciplinary Processes 77
- Where Do Background Investigations Come In? 77
- Disciplinary Processes 78
    - Termination of Employment 79
- Best Practices: The Bottom Line 81

Chapter Eight: Best Practices: Gig Workers and Contractors 83
- Policies and Procedures 83
    - Onboarding 84
    - Your Gig Handbook 84
    - Clarity in Position 85
    - Term Lengths 86
    - Culture, Core Values, and Mission 86
    - Company Policies and Disciplinary Processes 87
- Where Do Background Investigations Come In? 88
- Disciplinary Processes 89
    - Termination of Gig Workers 90
- Best Practices: The Bottom Line 91

Chapter Nine: Post-Hire Challenges 93
- Direct Post-Employment Challenges 93
- Course-of-Employment Challenges 95
    - Establishing Protocols 96
- Post-Hire Challenges in Summary 98

Chapter Ten: Avoiding Litigation 99
- Litigation: Example Cases 99
    - 1. The Target Case 99
    - 2. The U.S. Census Bureau 100
    - 3. The Frito Lay Case 100

Why This Happens	101
What Can Be Done Differently?	101
1. An Annual Audit of Current Processes	102
2. Following Best Practices	102
3. HR Compliance	104
Chapter Eleven: Best Practices by Industry	**107**
The Finance/Banking Sector	107
The Technology Sector	109
The Energy Sector	110
The Gaming and Hospitality Sector	111
The Transportation Sector	112
The Staffing Sector	113
The Healthcare Sector	115
Chapter Twelve	**117**
Summary and Closing	117
About the Author	**121**

Introduction

I have investigation in my blood. And that's not an overstatement. An early memory I have is being twelve years old and following a subject into a shopping mall to trace their movements. And we're not talking the male Nancy Drew here; this wasn't a fantasy fueled by too much Scooby Doo. I was working.

Let me explain. My mom and dad were private investigators. For as long as I can remember, investigation has been a part of my life. Dinnertime chats, ride-alongs with my parents, even the occasional sleuthing job like the one at the mall. And for as long as I can remember, I've loved it.

It's easy to throw words like "justice" and "fairness" around, but when I was a kid I had real-world examples of both of these. Before long, I was working with Mom and Dad after school and on weekends. I did surveillance, located witnesses, went undercover, conducted background checks, and even met with clients. All before I was old enough to apply for a driver's license.

It was a dream job for a teenage boy, and I'm honestly not overstating when I say I have investigation in my blood. So it was only natural that after high school I went to SUNY Albany to study criminal justice. I eventually graduated with a double major: a BS in criminal justice and a BA in Italian. The Italian was simply because it was my second language at home and something I enjoyed.

With my degree in hand and over fifteen years of experience as a private investigator with my parents' company, in 2005 I founded Alliance Worldwide Investigative Group. My company and I work with all kinds of organizations, managing risks from an investigative perspective. On an average day we can run background checks for pre-hiring, help in a fraud investigation, or track down an insurance scammer. It's all my boyhood dreams come true, and a life that I truly love.

After over a decade, Alliance has become a company that works both nationally and internationally to help organizations up their bottom line and manage all the challenges associated with "human capital," or employees.

Personally, I have over 2,500 hours of field investigative work under my belt, from asset investigations to background checks, locating missing witnesses to skip tracing. I also take part in forums and presentations using my experience to talk about best practices in the investigative industry. I am a board member of many industry organizations as well as non-profits, and have been featured in both local and national media. I am seen as an industry expert, conduct lectures, and have been honored as an Outstanding Business Person.

In short: investigation really *is* in my blood. That's me, but why am I introducing myself to you? Because I think I can help you. No, I *know* I can help you.

Investigation and Human Resources

"Human capital" or employees are at the heart of any organization. People are, without a doubt, the most important part of a company. However, I don't think I'm telling you anything new when I say that people aren't always honest.

Anyone who works in human resources will tell you that HR is not an easy life. Dealing with people, their mistakes, their personalities, their foibles, is not easy. Add in to this the fact that people don't always tell the truth, and you can see why working in HR is stressful.

The consequences of making a mistake in hiring can be big, which is why this book is titled *Avoiding Costly Hiring Mistakes*. Once you've hired someone, anything that person has (or hasn't) done can not only reflect on your business's reputation, but may also impact your bottom line.

Don't believe me? What if that new hire in the finance department doesn't actually have the finance degree they claim to have? What if that squeaky-clean resume from a new personal assistant hides a criminal record for theft? We don't have to talk only about big, dramatic incidents. Perhaps you have a small company and have chosen a candidate for a job because you think he's a good fit, his CV lists hobbies and experiences that you think will make him a great team member. But those hobbies and experiences don't end up being real, and you end up with an employee who doesn't fit into your company ethic. So you need to go through the process of firing and re-hiring, which is both costly and time consuming.

By some estimates, half of all resumes are based on a lie. Online services have made it easier than ever to produce not only a great-looking CV, but also online evidence to back up that CV. These services can do everything from ensuring you have a degree certificate that you didn't earn to creating web pages for companies that don't exist so you can claim you worked there, and even setting people up with fake followers on social media. And this evidence is convincing. Trust me, I see it every day.

Making bad hires isn't just a question of companies not running background checks anymore; it's a question of not running the right checks, not doing all the due diligence. Which is where I come in. I know how to run that due diligence, and by passing that knowledge on to you I can save you time, money, and even the reputation of your company.

The best way to avoid problems with a bad hire is to not make that bad hire in the first place, and that's why I'm here to help you.

The Bottom Line

HR investigation is an important part of any hiring process, but it can be one fraught with difficulties. From the challenges of navigating potentially false online leads to the legalities of running background checks, investigation isn't always simple. In this book you'll learn:

- How to evaluate the costs of a bad hire and manage risks associated with hiring not just employees but also freelancers and gig workers

- How to evaluate potential employees from resumes and the interview process

- How to run appropriate background checks legally and effectively

- How to do your due diligence once you've committed to hiring

- How to put in place the best practices for hiring, including processes not only for employees but also for the rapidly growing sector of gig workers and for subcontractors too

- How to avoid potential legal issues

And lots, lots more. If you want to ensure that you're hiring the right person with the right qualifications in the right manner, then everything you need to know is right here. The only thing you need to do is turn the page and start reading.

Chapter One

The Definition of Risk in the Employment World

Risk is part of running any company or organization, something that should be news to no one in the business world. But as an employer, much of your risk centers around the human element, which is something that can be difficult to calculate. Simply employing people adds a huge level of risk to your business. In today's world there are more ways than ever to employ people, whether that's traditional employment, contracting, or gig workers. And each of these areas comes with its own kind of risk. In addition, there are risks associated less directly with employment but that are still important concerns.

The Risk of Employment

The average American will spend 90,000 hours at work during their lifetime. Of course, that average includes part-time workers, as well as those who take significant amounts of time off for things like maternity leave and disability, so the actual number of hours the real American will work over a lifetime is probably a lot more than that. As an employer, you're responsible for somewhere around a third of an employee's life, depending on how long they work for you. And rather obviously, there are a lot of things that can go wrong during that time period. The risks rise, however, as employee fit diminishes.

The largest risk taken in a traditional employment situation is that of hiring. Making the wrong decision can have a huge impact on your business. The process of hiring a worker (whether an employee or a contractor) is time consuming and costly. Those time and financial investments increase whenever a bad hire is made. But what is the actual cost of making a bad hire?

The Cost of a Bad Hire

It's difficult to put an actual dollar number on the cost of hiring, since much depends on the kind of position you're hiring for and the kind of company you are. The cost may be a few bucks to place an online ad for a new janitor, or the cost may be as high as a quarter of a million dollars for large companies filling specialized positions that require recruitment. There are several factors that need to be taken into account when calculating how much a hire costs you:

- Advertising and recruitment costs: including things like hiring fairs, online advertisements, flying in applicants for interviews, and the like

- Employee time: the paid time others spend interviewing and selecting candidates

- Relocation costs: depending on the candidate and his location, relocation packages can be very costly indeed

- Training costs: integrating and learning costs both for the new employee and for those responsible for training

- Negative impact costs: including things like impacted team performance as employee changeover occurs, disruption to ongoing projects, customers who may be lost during the changeover time frame, and other less tangible costs

- Litigation fees: which may be necessary both for "good" and "bad" hires, depending on the situation they were hired into.

The above can be defined as "hiring costs." And, of course, there are a multitude of other expenses that could appear on this list. For example, there's the issue of a bad cultural fit. Your organization has a corporate culture, but what happens when a hiree doesn't fit into that culture? When an employee is a bad cultural fit, not meeting the core values of the company (perhaps not meeting that "passion for excellence" core value, for example), you potentially lose clients, and therefore money. And the flip side of that is that the employee him- or herself may be unhappy, which leads to decreased productivity. Happy employees mean efficient and productive ones, which in turn means happy customers.

But what if that hire doesn't go as planned? The cost of a bad hire includes all of the above, plus the salary paid to the bad hire while he or she is working, plus severance pay, plus any costs associated with disruption of business or mistakes/failures of the bad hire.

While putting an actual dollar amount on the cost of a bad hire is something that can't be generalized, the bottom line here is that a bad hire costs both time and money that your business can't afford.

There are, of course, other risks associated with employees: corporate espionage, decline in performance, and all sorts of other things we will touch upon later. But that initial hiring risk is the biggest, and one that shouldn't be overlooked.

Other Employment Scenarios

Not all companies nowadays engage in a traditional employer-employee relationship. In fact, gig working and subcontracting are more common than ever. Generally, this is to do with reasons of economy. When done correctly (legally, and with due diligence), both gig working and subcontracting can save companies vast amounts of money. But these both bring with them their own kinds of risk.

Gig Workers

By 2020 almost half of the US workforce is predicted to be some kind of freelance worker. The benefits of hiring gig workers are clear. As an employer, you don't have to pay benefits, accede to certain labor laws (such as minimum wage laws), and for the most part won't be paying overhead (since the majority of gig workers are remote). The risks of hiring gig workers may be less clear, and there are a couple of considerations here.

A Gig Worker Must NOT Be an Employee

By far the biggest risk in hiring a gig worker is that there is, as yet, no clear differentiation between what qualifies as a gig worker and what qualifies as an employee. The gig-working economy has expanded far faster than US labor law has changed. This has resulted in no clear definition of the label "gig worker." As an employer hiring a gig worker, you take the risk that that worker may then try to claim employee status, and the courts may well side with them. We have seen this in court cases involving major corporations, and this legal gray area is a worrying risk when legal costs, backpay of benefits, and company reputation are on the line.

In determining whether a worker is an employee or not, courts look at a variety of factors. These include the length of the working relationship, the permanence of such a relationship, whether the worker uses independent business judgment, the number of hours worked, the tasks required, and many other factors.

Whether or not someone is a gig worker is not a question I'm qualified to answer, and I would suggest legal advice if you are in any doubt, but this is a risk that you, as an employer, must understand when contracting work out to independent contractors.

Gig Workers Present Cyber Concerns

The other major risk inherent in hiring anyone who works remotely, and which applies mostly to gig workers, is that of cyber safety. With remote workers logging in from unknown sources, your IT infrastructure is placed under threat. This could be as simple as needing to pass along secure passwords to an independent programmer who may need to work on your systems, or as complex as someone else hacking into a gig worker's system and using that to gain access to your systems.

In a brick-and-mortar business the IT infrastructure is under company control. Which antivirus programs you run, which files are accessible from outside the company intranet, and so on are all determined by the company. When using gig workers, you lack control in this area, and the consequences can be devastating.

Subcontractors

Outsourcing work to staffing agencies or other third parties is another common way of cost cutting in the modern business world. Whether that's temps, janitorial staff, or IT and cyber security workers, getting specialized companies to perform specialized tasks means the business as a whole can save money. But there is one overwhelming risk in handling employment in this fashion.

You Subcontract Everything

Subcontracting may be a temporary or a permanent solution to a company's staffing issues, but either way, the risk remains the same. By subcontracting work you are subcontracting everything. That may seem blindingly obvious—of course you're subcontracting everything; that's the whole point of the exercise. But what you may not have considered is that you're also subcontracting vetting. By employing a third party to organize hiring and jobs getting done, you are also depending on the fact that that third party appropriately vets anyone they're about to send to your premises.

You're effectively bypassing your own company-wide vetting policy, whatever that may be, and allowing someone else to decide who is qualified to enter your company door.

As employers we often spend a lot of time, energy, and money on ensuring that those we hire are appropriately qualified (in a security sense of the word) to come onto our premises. We question the criminal history of employees, and we try to minimize security risks. But then we think nothing of buzzing the pizza delivery guy, or the janitor, or the new temp into the building.

Not only that, but the fact that we're used to seeing "new faces" (since many subcontracting companies use a variety of workers, rather than one "familiar face" to fill a role) means that we're less likely to question a stranger walking into a building like they belong there.

Subcontracting work may have financial benefits, but it also has security risks, and ones that shouldn't be overlooked.

How Do We Manage This in the Organization?

Whether you're hiring gig workers or subcontracting, how should an organization manage the individual risks that are presented? We will look at this in more detail in later chapters. But for now, being aware of the risks that are inherent in hiring either of these options is a good start. And ensuring that processes are in place to treat gig workers and subcontractors in a different (and more appropriate) way than employees is key.

Obviously, you must operate under the law, whichever laws apply in the situation you're dealing with. But you must also have company-wide processes in place to deal with potential issues with each of the three groups of workers we have discussed: employees, gig workers, and subcontractors.

Overall Company-Wide Risks

In addition to directly worker-related risks, there are other company-wide risks that must also be taken into consideration. Again, we'll look at these in more detail later. However, these risks fall into these general areas:

1. Physical/Workplace Risks

These are the risks associated with the workplace itself that are by their nature connected to the "people element" of the company. How easy is a building to access? How is access controlled? Who can access the workplace or parts thereof? The physical premises of a workplace are often not as secure as one might presume. Partners of employees, "rides," food delivery services, and other delivery services, all may gain easy access to workplaces. But that guy in the FedEx uniform might not actually work for FedEx. That employee partner might be an ex with a restraining order. In these kinds of cases, how easy would it be for someone who is "security unqualified" to walk into the workplace?

Physical security is a risk, and one that encompasses all kinds of consequences from active shooter situations to corporate espionage and beyond.

2. Cyber Risks

Cyber threats are ever present in today's world. How safe is your company's IT infrastructure? How observant are your cyber security specialists? What processes are put in place to not only ensure that hacking doesn't happen, but to control responses if it does? And, as always when the human element is present, are employees appropriately trained in cyber security? Do they know how to use cyber security tools? Do they know how to do something as simple as creating a secure password?

Risks involving the cyber world can be difficult to assess, since it's a world that is constantly evolving and changing. And yet having processes in place to deal with cyber threats can help minimize those risks.

3. Social Risks

The area of social risks is a murky one, but one that must be considered. How well trained are your staff members to deal with other people? Do they know what information they are allowed to distribute, and what must remain a company secret? Are they trained to understand what social engineering is and how to recognize it? Are they savvy enough to avoid discussing things that, even tangentially, may help someone infiltrate the company?

In order to illustrate better this nebulous social concept, let me use an example that happened to me recently. One of my colleagues received an email purportedly from me asking her to transfer a large amount of money into a certain bank account. Fortunately, she was well trained and when carefully reading the email determined that the writing style was simply not mine, so before transferring money, she called me to ascertain whether or not I truly wanted her to do so.

All kinds of social risks were present here. Somebody knew enough about me (potentially by a method as simple as calling and asking reception for me, or overhearing a conversation) to know that I was out of town, and therefore more likely to send an email with such a request rather than asking directly; to be able to create an email account that looked as though it belonged to me; and to contact the appropriate person (my colleague) who was able to transfer funds. Taken individually, any of these things (my business trip, my full name, the role of my colleague in the company) may not be seen as privileged information. And yet as a whole they could have potentially added up to something that cost my company a fair amount of money.

The social risks of working with people are constant, and should not be underestimated.

What Does a Breach Cost Your Organization?

There are risks in hiring, risks in working with gig workers and subcontractors, risks to having physical premises, risks involved in cyberspace, and social risks inherent in working with people. But what are the potential costs of running afoul of all these risks?

The cost runs the gamut. Perhaps it's the theft of five dollars in petty cash that an opportunistic thief takes from an open desk drawer. Perhaps it's physical harm and even death if a bomber or shooter is allowed access to a building (either because he or she works there or because physical security allows them to slip through). Perhaps it's a multi-million-dollar lawsuit. Perhaps it's the headache of having to fire an employee and hire someone else. Perhaps it's the folding of a once prosperous company.

Whatever the cost, there are ways to minimize all these risks. So let us first turn to what is for most companies a major source of risk: that of hiring new employees.

Chapter Two

Talent & Hiring Process

We've established that the human factor in an organization is an understandable risk, and that hiring new employees is a risk, but are there ways in which this liability can be mitigated? There are, of course, laws that impact hiring, as well as best practices, and even company-wide processes. So yes, that risk can be (and often is) mitigated. But is it being mitigated in the best possible way? Are you lowering that risk as much as it's possible to do so? The answer to that depends upon how your hiring process works, and whether or not you're compliant with the myriad of laws and best practices involving onboarding new hires.

Recruitment and Selection

The initial step in any hiring process is locating the talent pool. Locating the talent that you need to fill a role is not only exceptionally important, but is also an ever-changing process. In the past, word of mouth, friends of friends, perhaps a notice in a window or an ad in a newspaper were enough to get the talent you needed knocking on your door. Nowadays, things are obviously a little different.

Though word of mouth and networking do still play a role, these days we're more likely to use slightly more high-tech recruiting methods. Online job boards are probably the most obvious solution, sites that collate resumes and allow you to more easily direct a job posting to those qualified to apply for it. Applicant Tracking Systems (ATS) are also becoming more and more common. An ATS is a software application that essentially sorts through resumes received in order to narrow down the choices to candidates who are a best fit for the role that's open.

Once you have a list of your top candidates, you're looking to narrow down that choice even more. Often this happens in an interview process, perhaps an hour or two, after which a candidate is hired. Let's back up a second here. You've had a resume that may have been picked from the herd by a recruitment manager or software application. You've had a one- or two-page summary of someone's experience. You've spent perhaps an hour or two with that person, maybe? And now that person is about to become a part of your organization with access to all the assets involved in that. Are you seeing red flags right now? You should be. The general, normal process of recruiting and hiring described above hasn't exactly done much to mitigate the risk of making a bad hire. So let's talk solutions here.

The Interview Process

For every position there are potentially thousands of applicants. They all complete an application, and then we're supposed to bring one of them on board while knowing what is, technically, very little about them. Sifting through the resumes and applications and identifying the best fits can often be done these days with one of the above-mentioned Applicant Tracking Systems, or by a keen-eyed recruitment manager. Of course, anyone can write anything on paper, and that's something we'll get back to later when discussing background checks. But for now, let's assume you have winnowed down your thousands of applications and found several that are worthy of at least an initial interview.

The interview is the first time you really get to meet a candidate and identify whether they truly are the fit you believed they could be on paper. And yet hiring managers are so pressed to hire and get their jobs done quickly that in many instances a mere half hour is granted to them to determine whether or not a candidate is fit for a purpose. In order to mitigate the risk of a new hire, though, there are several components that should be looked at during the interview process. And when going through these components it should become obvious that thirty minutes really isn't enough time to get the job done properly. So what should we be looking for during this interview process?

Our goal is to narrow down the already narrowed field of candidates to two, three, or four solid candidates to take on to the next stage. In order to do this, there are four steps that must be gone through:

Determining Culture/Personality Fit

This is an area in which many hirers slip up. In chapter one we discussed how a good culture fit is important in an employee. A potential employee must fit into the corporate culture and share, or be willing to share, a company's core values. And yet many companies do not have a process for determining this during an interview.

Obviously, we can draw certain conclusions from certain kinds of behavior. If a candidate comes across as arrogant or rude during an interview for a role where he or she is likely to be working with the public or in a close-knit team, his or her personality traits are unlikely to make for a good fit. But things aren't always this clear cut.

To determine a good fit, it's good practice to ask behavior-based questions that apply to the qualities you're looking for. This is something we do in our company and is an effective method for ensuring that a candidate is a good fit for your core values. If, for example, one of your company's core values is excellence, you might ask: "Tell me about a time at a previous job where you went above and beyond." Or in the case of hiring to fulfill a role where good teamwork is essential, you may ask: "Tell me about a time when you worked in a team. How successful were you? How successful was the team? What role did you play in that team?"

This is a simple technique that is a good way of digging deeper into a candidate's background, corporate values, and attitude.

Determining Skills

Which skills are necessary to fulfill a role are dependent on the role in question. But a skills assessment is always a good way of ensuring that a candidate is capable of doing what they claim they can, or of being trained to do what is necessary. This could be as simple as a typing test, or may involve more complex things such as role playing the lead of a negotiation. It could be practical, or may be based on knowledge and questioning. However, it is essential that a candidate's skills are tested in some way. Again, anyone can write anything on a piece of paper, but until you see those skills in practice you can't know for sure that the candidate possesses them.

Determining Physical Health

This may or may not be necessary, depending upon the role in question. But in some positions it is essential that a candidate is physically fit enough to fulfill that position. Company policies vary on this, as do legal requirements, but a full physical may form a part of the interview process.

Determining Other Elements

Finally, you may also need to determine other things, again dependent on the position to be filled. This final stage is highly variable and can encompass a vast range of things such as ability and willingness to travel, for example. A candidate with a fear of flying is hardly likely to be able to make a cross-coast meeting once a week. In essence, this section is for determining anything that you know is essential to the role that has not already been covered in prior sections. You want to know as much as possible about the candidates being interviewed, and whether you and your company choose to question ability to travel or hold psychological testing, or anything in between, everything you can learn about your candidates will lessen the eventual risk of hiring them.

The Finalists

After a solid interview process you should be left with a handful of candidates who fulfill your requirements, at which point we move into background screening. Some companies choose to go forward in the process with one solid candidate, while others gather the top three or four and run checks on all of them. In general, the latter of these two options is more advisable.

Yes, running backgrounds on three or four candidates is more costly and time consuming; however, the advantages are significant. As the employer, you have the ability to properly vet all candidates and make an effective hiring decision not merely hinged upon the background investigation. Let's say that there is some information that is developed in comparing multiple candidates' results. The employer now has options, whereas by simply running one candidate, their hands are tied and they face the potential of being discriminatory. For example, information from a reference may tell an employer a different story about their work ethic. This information may not be impactful enough to make an adverse decision, but having two other candidates to draw from without the same issue, all things equal, would involve a more beneficial outcome. There could be other reasons why the other candidates are more qualified for the role, and leaving it up to just the background investigation can be problematic.

Background Investigation Time

The bottom line now is that the only way you're going to find out as much as you need to know about your potential employees is by running a background investigation. Depending on the business you're in, a comprehensive background check may be a legal obligation. Leaving the processes and laws behind for a moment, what kind of things should you be interested in finding out?

Many people think of a background "check" (we like to use the word "investigation" because it signifies a true investigation vs. a check) as a criminal-history check, and that's simply not the case. Though a criminal history does form a part of a background investigation, there are many other elements involved. There's a long list of elements that should be of interest (though whether or not you can get hold of the necessary information is another matter):

- **Character:** This should be self-explanatory; a person's character can say a lot about how they will fit in with a company's ethos and how well they may work with others. However, character is one of the toughest elements to thoroughly cover in someone's background. Social media can provide some idea of a candidate's character, as may references, but this is probably the biggest gray area when it comes to what can be found out and how reliable found information may be.

- **Financial:** This is an ever-changing landscape. Use of someone's financial background must be directly related to their core job duties. In years past, employers would arbitrarily include "credit checks" as part of a background investigation without a justifiable purpose. Times have changed, and now, as of the writing of this book, there are a number of states that make the use of credit reports in the hiring process illegal unless explicitly job related. As a matter of fact, there is a federal-level bill that has been introduced to attempt to make the use of credit reports illegal in the employment and hiring decision. In general, credit reports are discriminatory and subjective and leave the interpretation up to the user, which has caused many applicants challenges. There are some great alternatives to this that tell the same story but are non-discriminatory (bankruptcies, liens, and judgments).

- **Criminal:** Probably the most obvious element, and the element that most people consider when running a background check. Does the candidate have a criminal history? Outstanding warrants? Court proceedings coming up against them? In a handful of industries this will not matter, but in the majority of companies (particularly when assets and trust are involved) a criminal history can automatically invalidate a candidate. There are many levels of criminal background investigations including local (city/town/village), county-wide, state-wide, and federal. Understanding how each search is conducted and what is available will result in a beneficial outcome.

- **Sex Offender Registry:** Has the candidate been entered onto the registry? If so, this could mean an automatic disqualification from the hiring process, particularly if the candidate is to be working in the vicinity of children. Understanding that there are multiple levels and accessing each level is a critical part of the process.

- **Social and Social Media:** This is a growing area of interest in the world of background checks. As social media becomes more prevalent, it can help to form a fuller picture of a candidate. Posted pictures of a weekend spent volunteering are likely to form a better impression than pictures of a weekend spent drinking and partying. In some cases, information from social media may be enough to convince you that a candidate is unsuitable, but beware it is not that cut and dry.

- **Employment:** A candidate has almost certainly already provided you with a list of prior employers via his resume or application. It's at this point that those claims should be checked out. Did he or she really work for whom they listed? Did they really fulfill the role they claim to have filled? What was their reason for leaving the employ of that company?

- **Education:** Similarly, you probably already have information from the candidate about where and to what level he or she was educated. Again, those claims need to be checked out. Did they really attend the stated institution? Did they really graduate? Do they have the degree they claim to hold?

- **References:** Again, a candidate's claims need to be checked out. Who are the references he or she has listed? Are those references suitably placed to provide information about the candidate? Are those references who the candidate claims them to be?

- **Technical Ability:** Depending on the role to be filled, a candidate may be claiming proficiency in some technical area or areas. Are those claims true? Can he or she really do what he or she claims? The candidate's future ability to perform his or her role may depend on this.

- **And More:** There may be other areas that a background check may investigate, depending on the client's needs, the company's wishes, and the background of the actual investigator. For example, if an applicant claims certain physical limitations that would hinder some parts of his or her performance, those may be thoroughly checked out. Voluntary service may also be checked. Basically, anything that the candidate claims that could be doubted can be subject to investigation in a background check.

Is This Going Too Far?

You may be wondering at this point if all of this information is really necessary, if perhaps we're taking things too far. The truth is that we actually have no way of knowing how many applicants lie on their resumes. According to SHRM (the Society for Human Resource Management) anywhere between 40% and 70% of candidates falsify at least portions of their resumes. Those are huge percentages. On a personal note, my company tends to average between 10% and 12% hit (adverse findings) rate in spotting resume falsifications during background checks. The most common falsifications we see are:

- **Degrees:** Claiming a degree that the candidate did not earn, or claiming to have attended an institution that has no record of the candidate.

- **Dates of Employment:** Claiming to have worked for a company or companies when either the company in question has no record of the candidate, or dates on company records do not match (often done to hide gaps in employment history).

- **Salary History:** Claiming to have earned more in an attempt to bump up a salary offer from a potential new employer.

There are many other kinds of falsification that we see on resumes. Skill stretching is claiming to possess skills that the candidate actually doesn't have, or doesn't have adequate experience in. Falsifying military service, claiming to be a veteran when the candidate is not, is another one.

These numbers should tell you that lying on paper is common enough that we absolutely should be running background checks. And when we consider the potential cost of a bad hire, the cost of running background checks on several candidates pales in comparison. Inflating job titles, claiming language fluency, providing fake addresses, all are common lies. And if that weren't enough, there are services available online that will provide a candidate with a very professional-looking and believable resume that makes them look perfect for a role for a hefty fee. Those resumes are completely fabricated, though in many cases are backed up with websites and answering services that under cursory examination more than hold up.

On top of all of this, there are nowadays some questions that we are no longer allowed to ask on employee applications. In some 25 states, for example, fair-hiring policies now dictate that employers cannot ask candidates if they have ever been convicted of a crime on a job application. This means that there is potentially important information that cannot simply be gained by asking, whether or not you can trust the candidate's response. All of this leads us to a big question.

If They're Lying About X, What Else Are They Lying About?

A background check might reveal a small fabrication. Perhaps the candidate attended a two-year degree program, rather than the four-year program they claim to have attended. Perhaps they didn't work for company Y for the eighteen months they claimed, but only for sixteen months. Maybe they're not quite as fluent in French as they've led you to believe.

In some cases, these fabrications may directly impact future job performance; in others, not so much. But the essential problem is that if a candidate is caught lying about one thing, what else are they lying about? Can that candidate henceforth be trusted to be truthful? Not just in the other claims they have made during the application process, but also moving forward in the role they hope to fill.

In a way, a background check helps to gauge that "gray area" of character that we mentioned above. Whether or not the falsifications uncovered will impact job performance, the lack of character shown in making the falsification in the first place is worrying for a potential employer.

So much for why background checking is necessary. But what is the actual process? That's where we'll turn next.

Not All Background Checks Are Created Equal

There are really two kinds of background checks that can be performed: private sector checks and public sector checks. Private sector checks are generally done for companies, while public sector checks are performed for those who want to work in or have exposure to the public sector (think school teachers, bus drivers, some healthcare/hospital jobs). These two kinds of background checks are different not only in process but also in efficacy, though both have their pros and cons. For example, a private sector check is not allowed to ask for a candidate's fingerprints to compare against government databases. So let's first take a look at the difference between a private sector and a public sector background check.

1. Private Sector Background Checks

We will go into more depth about private sector background checks and how they're run in later pages. However, the basics go like this: A candidate first signs a release form and is given a series of other documents to review/sign in accordance with local/state/federal laws. The investigative team processes the appropriate investigation and determines the level of screening to be conducted. There are several types depending on the nature of the position and requirements. While most investigations involve conducting criminal searches, there are many more aspects to an individual's background that are typically investigated. There are far too many to list here, but some of the most common include: address history, credentials, credit, education, employment, identity, and more.

Going back to the criminal convictions research, the process can be complicated depending on the level of searches needed (misdemeanor or felony) and the extent to which an employer seeks to conduct true due-diligence (budget is a factor at times). Most criminal records are indexed in the appropriate-level court (local, county, state, federal) and the process for each varies depending on jurisdiction. In some cases, a manual in-person search is required (court runners are typically used) and in other cases the process is automated and direct access to courts is available from the background screening firm's offices. A myriad of other processes are typically followed, but ultimately it is the compilation of the searches together in a comprehensive format that forms the basis of a private sector background check.

Depending on the employer, we're looking for felonies and misdemeanors here, as well as anything else that stands out. A private sector check will follow a consistent methodology (meaning it will be done in the same way for each candidate and for each role to be filled) and use proper, legal processes. Court documents are the only effective tool to uncover any possible criminal records (vs. a fingerprint check, which is typically incomplete information lacking a final disposition.) As an employee, a private sector check also has advantages.

In the private sector, a candidate can challenge information found in a background check, just like you might challenge a credit report. The Fair Credit Reporting Act governs background investigations just as it does credit checks, which means a candidate can refute any findings that he or she believes to be unfair, untrue, or just plain wrong. If the candidate can provide proof to back up their refutation, then the background check firm (commonly referred to as a CRA—consumer reporting agency) must further review the matter and, if information is found to be inaccurate, is legally obligated to change the content. In short, a private sector background check gives candidates more rights and more protection.

For an employer, the advantages of a private sector background check are that the methodology is consistent and followed each and every time, there are fewer loopholes than with public sector checks, and court documents are the most up-to-date way to get information about any legal problems or proceedings against an applicant.

2. Public Sector Background Checks

In the public sector, methods are more variable. How a check is done and the processes involved may depend on what kind of public sector job is being applied for. Even then, the process may not always be followed, and due diligence may not always be consistent. There are plenty of loopholes in the public sector checking system, meaning that information is not always accurate or effective.

In the public sector the general process is that a candidate's fingerprints are taken and these are then run through the FBI and/or state system to pull up any adverse records tied to a possible subject. However, the problem here is that because investigators aren't going directly to the source (the court documents) they're getting second-hand information. The arrest record that's accessed through the FBI or other state system may not have been updated by the court, for example, and therefore shows out-of-date or incomplete information. Plus, there are no candidate rights in the public background checking process (unlike in the private sector process). All of this means that a public background check could end up ruling out a candidate unfairly, while a private sector check is less likely to do so.

On the other side, public sector checks do have access to more information than private sector checks, simply because the process is already being performed under government auspices. Though how dependable that information is depends very much on the process being followed, the process being consistent, and there being no loopholes in the process.

How Things Used to Be

How background checks are run, how employees are hired or not hired, is governed by strict laws and processes. However, things weren't always this way. Up until around 2000, background checks were mostly run by security in the private sector. HR (or Personnel, as it was then generally called) had little to do with this part of the hiring process. Security may or may not be made up of ex–police officers, but whatever their background, it was their job to sift through applications and determine whether or not an applicant was suitable. There were no laws about discriminatory hiring practices. Human Resources became involved only at the end of this process when security told them whom they could and could not hire based on whatever background checking had been done.

This presented some problems. Improper decisions were made due to a lack of legal guidelines for security to follow. Discrimination occurred, again due to lack of laws and guidelines. Security did not get back to unsuccessful candidates, so there could be no recourse if a candidate was unfairly withdrawn from the pool of applicants. Security personnel were rarely questioned about their decision or how they came to their decisions.

Obviously, this old process had many flaws. It was discriminatory and unfair. But then the laws began to change....

How Things Are Now

Obviously, this process has changed quite remarkably in recent years. These days, HR manages the entire recruitment process with only limited involvement by security. Not only that, but strict protocols have been developed in order to ensure that the hiring process is non-discriminatory and fair. In order to comply with these new protocols, it's essential that the hiring process considers the below policies and procedures both for running background checks and for the actual process of winnowing down the applicant field. There are six stages that should be gone through:

1. Application

Initially, the application form itself must be compliant with all laws both state and federal. This includes complying with the above-mentioned Fair Chance Act where applicable. Consider that there are questions that you may no longer be able to ask (such as criminal conviction history or salary history, for example) in the application part of the recruiting process. Questions relating to sex, race, disabilities, or other discriminatory factors that do not impact job performance cannot be included in either the application form or during the interview. It's highly advisable to read up on current EEOC (Equal Employment Opportunity Commission) guidelines as well as any relevant state laws.

2. Release Form

Before a background check can be run, a candidate must sign a release form. Again, the details of this form will vary depending on state laws; however, it is essential that permission is given in writing for a check to go ahead. A release form is required in order to be compliant with FCRA (the Fair Credit Reporting Act). A suitable release form should also set the groundwork for any future background checks to be run in the case of promotion, for example, or even annual review.

3. Disclosure

Applicants must also sign a notice of disclosure, again in order to be compliant with FCRA. This states that a full background check is to be done and that the candidate has the right to request a copy of the full report. In addition, they are provided with a Summary of Rights under the FCRA.

4. Other Documents

Depending on your location and your organizational needs, there may be further document requirements. These documents will depend on the role in question as well as on local laws.

One great example of an additional document is an SSA-89. This form allows for CBSV (Consent Based Social Security Number Verification). A CBSV search will verify an applicant's social security number, name, date of birth, and gender, and is useful in assuring that no identity theft has taken place. However, without that additional release form, a CBSV search cannot be done. Extra consent forms are also required for things like income tax return verification from the IRS. Depending on the information you need, you may require many more documents than an initial release form.

5. International Issues

In a world that's rapidly growing smaller, international issues also have to be considered. In order to perform background checks outside of the US you will need to be in compliance with any local laws involved. It's important that whoever is running an international background check is fully familiar with these laws. GDPR and European data privacy laws are just one example of this.

6. Limitations

Finally, limitations must also be kept in mind. These include the limitations of any release signed, which may or may not allow you to find certain information, as well as limitations to documents themselves. In some cases it simply may not be possible to get the information you wish to know. In other cases, there may be issues outside of your (and your investigator's) control. Identity theft must be considered, for example. A background check does not reveal all, and in the case of identity theft it may not reveal anything pertinent at all.

The bottom line here is that there is a lot of protocol involved in staying compliant with hiring laws. These laws are not designed to make the recruiter's life more difficult; they're designed to provide fair and equal opportunity to applicants. However, the side effect of these laws is that legally recruiting and running background checks can be a very complicated procedure indeed.

A Contingent Offer?

Once the protocols are all up and running and the background checking process can begin, there is one essential question that arises. Do you make a job offer contingent on the background check? That is, do you say, "You have the job as long as the background check comes up clean"?

In general, a contingent offer is a bad idea. Firstly, this locks you into an agreement that you may not wish to keep. If, for example, a background check shows up something that you do not like and yet is not grounds for not hiring, you could be in trouble. Essentially, not giving a contingent offer is a sensible precaution in the same way that running background checks on multiple candidates rather than just one is a sensible precaution. It allows you to keep your options open.

There may be exceptions to this general rule, though. Some states do not allow a full background check to be run unless a contingent offer of employment has been given. So again, knowing your local laws regarding this issue is key.

The Results are In: To Hire or Not to Hire?

Once the background check results come in, that all-important decision needs to be made: are you going to hire or not? But this isn't simply a question of making a phone call or two. There are still additional concerns that need to be kept in mind depending on whether you've chosen to hire or not.

Hiring

If you've chosen to go with a candidate, then there are still a couple of things that may or may not be required before hiring. You'll need to think about whether there's anything else that you need to do or know before actually signing contracts.

The most common of these is drug testing. Again, state laws vary here, and you may or may not be permitted to test for intoxicants. You may only be able to test for intoxicants once a conditional job offer has been made. Processes also vary depending on state, so knowing the laws in your location is essential.

You may also want to consider requiring a physical, if you have not already done this, to prove that a potential employee is fit for work.

Not Hiring

Not hiring a candidate is an even more complex procedure than hiring. Initially, you must be sure that the reason you're choosing not to hire is valid. Though adverse findings may show up in a background check, these are not necessarily legal grounds not to hire. Your investigator should be able to advise you on this. But, just as an example, in some states you cannot use a criminal conviction that occurred over a pre-determined limit of time as reason to deny a candidate. Once you're sure you're compliant in your reasoning, there are then two stages to the process of declining a candidate:

1. Pre-Adverse Action

Before notice is given of non-employment, a candidate must first have an opportunity to defend himself and his rights. A notice of pre-adverse action basically says, "We're thinking of not hiring you due to information found during your background check." This notice allows the candidate time to view the background check report and to refute any instances they believe to be incorrect. It is recommended that the candidate be given ample time to respond to the notice; many employers allot 48–72 hours.

Should a candidate respond to this pre-adverse action notice, then you may find yourself delaying hiring until the problem can be solved. However, this is a necessary step in order to be FCRA compliant.

2. Adverse Action

Once a pre-adverse action notice has been sent and the appropriate amount of time has passed without the candidate refuting the background check, or should the candidate be unable to provide proof of his refutation, you may then send an adverse action notice. This basically says, "We have decided not to hire you based on your background check."

This may all seem like a lot of work just so that you can *not* hire a candidate; however, it is necessary to follow these formal steps in order to be legally compliant and avoid litigation. Not following these steps can result in lawsuits.

Mitigating Hiring Risks

The steps involved in recruiting and hiring a new employee while mitigating the risk of doing so and still remaining legally compliant are very complex. These processes and laws are also constantly changing, meaning it's important that your chosen investigator is up to date with his or her knowledge. However, the time taken and complexity of the issue are more than outweighed by the potential cost of a bad hire.

Thus far we've dealt with onboarding new employees. But as we discussed back in chapter one, more and more companies are choosing instead to deal with gig workers, subcontractors, and freelancers. So how do our risk mitigation processes differ when we turn away from traditional employees? That's the subject of our next chapter.

Chapter Three

Subcontractors, Gig Workers, and More

It used to be that an employer could count on his employees being, well, employees. But this is no longer the case. As the employment world changes, it's important that employers stay up to date when assessing risk that comes not just from the traditional employee role, but also from those workers who don't fall under the heading of "employees."

Other Employment Scenarios

In chapter one we briefly discussed the issue of alternative employment strategies. But let's briefly recap on that before we continue. The employment world is rapidly changing, with more and more companies (including major corporations) onboarding gig workers and subcontractors. The risks presented by these hiring solutions only vary slightly when compared to hiring more traditional employees.

There are many advantages to hiring gig workers and subcontractors. Lower overheads, lack of benefits to be paid, and fewer labor laws to be considered. All in all, hiring a non-traditional employee could be a solid economic decision for an employer. In fact, projections show that by the year 2020 almost half of workers in the US will be freelancers. This presents a rather unique set of problems when hiring and assessing risk.

The Unique Challenges of Non-Traditional Workers

First, and this pertains to both gig workers and subcontractors to some extent, the initial question has to be: Are these workers actually employees? You may think that's a rather obvious question to be asking, but you could be surprised. Though the employment world is changing, labor laws are not keeping up, and this can put companies in a legal gray area when hiring. There is as yet no clear definition of the term "gig worker" legally speaking. And this leads to the risk that someone hired as a freelancer may try to claim employee status in order to get benefits, for example. This is something that has happened, both in the US and abroad (in the case of Uber drivers, for example), and is not an overstated risk. Federal law dictates that employees must be treated and compensated in a certain way. Should a worker claim (and win) employee status, the consequences can be high, including: legal costs, back pay of benefits, and claims from the IRS demanding taxes that should have been paid on the employee's behalf. Legally speaking, courts look for three determining factors as to whether someone is an employee (though this is a complex matter and legal counsel should certainly be sought if there is any doubt):

- The Common Law Test: Does the employer control the work process? (I.e., is the worker told specifically what to do?)

- The Economic Realities Test: Is the worker economically dependent on the employer? (I.e., is this the only job the worker could realistically hold at one time?)

- The Hybrid Test: A combination of the two above things.

Once it's been determined that a hire truly is a non-employee, there are further risks involved. Particularly with gig workers there's the issue of remote access, presenting cyber risks to a company. Accessing a company intranet from outside the corporation can be dangerous. While your company servers and computers may be well protected, you have no idea how protected a gig worker's connection may be.

When we're talking about subcontracting we're talking about a wide variety of different tasks. Janitors, basic staffing, maintenance workers, servicing firms, landlords—all mean that "strangers" are entering company premises. I use that word to mean people who are not technically "known" to a company, workers who probably have not gone through the more stringent security and background investigations that a normal employee would have gone through. Many companies have a tendency to let subcontractors slide through the cracks when it comes to evaluating risk when hiring, and may depend on a third party (a staffing agency or janitorial firm, for example) to thoroughly check out workers who will be on site. Obviously, this isn't ideal.

The bottom line here is that an employee, a gig worker, and a subcontractor all present different risk issues during the hiring process, which will impact how the screening process is handled.

Gig Workers, Subcontractors, and Contractors, Oh My!

For the purposes of this chapter we'll define the ideas of gig workers, subcontractors, and contractors. But please keep in mind that this isn't a definitive definition (because legally there really isn't one yet) and shouldn't be used to determine the status of your new hire. However, a working definition will allow us to better explain the process of securely investigating and hiring each kind of worker, so it is important in these terms. So, we'll define two different kinds of alternative workers:

- **Large Contractors:** These are service providers and companies that have employees. These can vary from janitorial companies, sanitation workers, electrical contractors, lawn and maintenance services, staffing agencies, and everything in between.
- **Small Contractors and Gig Workers:** These are generally one-person operations. Perhaps it's a social media consultant,

or an IT security specialist, but in this case we're dealing with a sole individual rather than a company.

When hiring either of these alternatives, there are issues that need to be dealt with, some pertaining to just one of the two groups, some to both.

Risk Factor Issues

Whether you're hiring from a large contractor, a small one, or getting a gig worker, your initial question has to be: How tolerant are you of potential risk? It should be made clear here that anyone coming on site presents a risk, and whether that person is a landscape worker, security consultant, or employed receptionist, that risk is the same. Somebody coming on site may cause harm, do damage, steal company secrets, and what effect would this have on your organization?

My initial point is that it doesn't matter whether we're talking about employees or contract workers—damage can still be done. Unfortunately, what so often happens is that once employees are out of the equation, procedures slip. HR may decide they no longer play a role, or security may decide that they are in control, once we're no longer talking about fixed employees. However, in truth both HR and security should be working together on this problem. And it *is* a problem. Nowadays in larger organizations there is a seat at the table for this—it's called risk management.

Any organization needs clear procedures to protect itself from the potential risk of people coming on site. Based on who is coming in, guidelines must be established surrounding what is and is not acceptable.

Should employees and contractors be screened in the same way? That will depend on what role a contractor is going to play, how often they will be in the building, and what kind of access they will have to products, customers, and locations. However, in essence, yes, a contractor can be treated in more or less the same way as a potential employee would be treated, with one important difference.

When looking to hire an employee, employers must comply with FCRA and EEOC regulations regarding discrimination and fair hiring. The same does not hold true when screening contract workers or gig workers. In part, this does make the screening process a little easier. However, it pays to be careful. Some states are now enacting legislation about third party background investigations and hiring processes, so again, legal advice is recommended and is location dependent.

This doesn't change the fact that there must be comprehensive and systematic procedures for all kinds of hiring. And most companies are now screening not only employees but also gig workers, and contract workers too. Is this necessary? Well, how much of a risk are you willing to run? With your company's financial future and reputation at stake, chances are you want to be as low risk as possible, which means screening. So let's first turn to issues surrounding larger contractors, service providers, and agencies.

Issues Surrounding Large Contractors

Many companies employ other companies to do work for them. Perhaps that's your tree guys, or your elevator maintenance men, or even a staffing agency to provide you with temps. In fact, there's a long list of potential contractors whom you could, and probably do, use. First, let's reiterate that FCRA guidelines do not apply to you here (they apply to the vendor company that hires the workers, not to the company hiring the vendor company).

In the case of large contracting companies there are two forms of investigation that you'll want to think about: investigation of the company itself, as well as investigation of any individual a company decides to send to your premises. Unfortunately, that second part is often overlooked. Yes, a vendor company may have its own investigative hiring procedures, but how do you know how stringent they are? How do you know if the vendor company has the same risk tolerance as you?

It's critical here that your first step is to check out the vendor. What do you know about them? What do you know about their screening processes for employees? A company *can* have a criminal record (as well as other adverse records), so the initial stage is to basically run a background investigation on the company itself. Once this is done, you can then enquire more closely about the actual persons who will come on site. It is perfectly fine, and in fact advisable, for you to run your own background investigation or screening on these people, despite the fact that they're actually employed by the vendor company.

And due to the fact that fair hiring rules and anti-discrimination laws for the most part aren't going to apply in these cases, it's also absolutely fine for you as a customer to dictate your own needs. You may say, for example, that you don't want anyone on site with a previous drug conviction (possibly important if you're a pharmaceutical company). More than that, you don't even have to give the vendor a reason why you don't want someone on site; you can simply ask for an alternative worker to be sent.

This is very different from an employee-employer relationship, where your hands are tied far more tightly. In this case, the onus lies with the vendor company. If you send someone off site, the vendor company will then need to deal with re-deploying that employee, or laying them off if there is no further work. You, on the other hand, bear no responsibility.

Knowing your minimum requirements for people coming on site, knowing your risk tolerance, and having procedures in place to ensure that you have all your bases covered, are all essential here, though you have more freedom than you would have when hiring an employee.

Issues Surrounding Gig Workers

If you're working with gig workers, or small one-person contracting companies, then the issues are slightly less complex. These workers are generally independent, are considered a 1099 for most companies, and often work other jobs simultaneously. However—and here's the important part—in essence they are no different from an employee when it comes to the risk perspective.

This means that when hiring gig workers, your risk assessment procedures should essentially be no different than if you were hiring an employee. The same standard background investigation, the same requirements, the same personnel involved. Your level of risk has not changed; therefore, the procedures already in place to combat that risk should also not change.

What Should You Do?

If you're hiring through a contractor, or hiring gig workers, what should your process be? I've already said that the risk is the same and therefore the process should also be the same, but let's take a brief look in more detail about what that process should be.

1. Establish Guidelines

Your first step is to establish guidelines for anyone other than an employee who is coming on site. These guidelines should be applied consistently and should also be consistent with your risk tolerance. Some companies may not allow non-employees to access certain areas (such as labs), for example, while others may allow full access but require an escort. You may require that a person coming on site has no drug convictions (again, perhaps you make pharmaceuticals), or no sex offender registry entries (perhaps there are children on site). The list can go on, and your guidelines will be dependent on your needs as a company.

These guidelines should also apply to how outside workers are treated. Do your employees know that the maintenance guys are required to wear ID badges? Do employees know that certain areas are secure and doors should not be held or propped open? Do reception workers know what questions to ask to determine whether someone should or should not be allowed on site?

A small, personal anecdote here to illustrate more exactly what I'm talking about: Several years ago I was in New York City and dropped by to visit a potential client. The client was not expecting me, but I thought I'd take the opportunity to make face-to-face contact. The receptionist on the ground floor asked if I was expected and I said no, so she called the client, who didn't answer. The receptionist decided to send me upstairs anyway, and a security guard put me in an elevator, but didn't accompany me. Once I was upstairs, a locked door was opened by an employee leaving who politely held the door open for me, allowing me inside. Once inside the actual office, I walked past several open and unlocked offices before finally tracking down my client.

Obviously, this was a huge security breech. Had I had nefarious inclinations, I could have stolen money, objects, or even trade secrets from my client's workplace and simply walked out. All because there were no appropriate guidelines in place to prevent me from doing so—or, if there were, those guidelines were not consistently applied.

2. Consider the Legal Guidelines

Again, you should also take legal advice for your particular state when making decisions, but do consider any potential legal obstacles or loopholes that may apply when hiring through a third party or a 1099 employee such as a gig worker.

3. Establish a Contract/Agreement

Establish a contract or agreement with your vendor company that clearly outlines your requirements for employees of that company to be on site. You may, for example, require that all their employees have a specific background investigation completed, carry ID badges, enter only certain parts of a building, or that they have a security escort when on the premises. These conditions will depend on you, but you have every right to demand them from your vendor company.

4. Ensure Your Status

Ensure that you are not the employer on record and that the vendor company is. As we discussed above, an employer has far more stringent responsibilities than someone who's simply hiring through a third party, so do ensure that you are not being put in the position of an employer.

It's essential that you have clear guidelines for what is and is not appropriate for workers on site. As a non-employer you have the right to terminate the relationship with any of these workers at any time, since you are not required to follow FCRA. Should someone be sent to your site who has not been properly vetted or who does not follow your requirements, then you are free to be rid of them as long as all your guidelines have been clear on what you expect.

It is not unusual for companies to run investigations on third-party employees such as contract workers or gig workers, and many firms have a checklist of investigations that they require before a person may come on site. Generally, these checklists include:

- Identity verification
- Criminal conviction status (all levels)
- References
- Employment history
- Education history
- Government sanctions and watch lists
- Sex offender registry check
- Other items, depending on the requirements of your business (for example, a certain amount of experience, or certain physical conditions)

In summary, just because you're hiring contractors or gig workers does not mean you no longer need to consider risk. In fact, for the most part, your risk management strategies should be very similar to those used when hiring employees. The laws may change, but the nature of the risk problem does not change; therefore, nor should your solutions change.

Thus far we've dealt with what happens before someone works for you. But what about once that job offer has been made and accepted? Risk management doesn't stop with the hiring process, and that is where we will turn next.

Chapter Four

Post-Employment Screening and Due Diligence

Having done your background investigations, come to an agreement, and signed your contracts, you might think that your job is done. You've got a fantastic new hire who you're confident is not only the best person for the job, but also has a clear background, so what more could you need to do? Though the majority of companies these days do perform some kind of pre-employment screening, many don't use post-employment screening—which could be a very costly mistake.

Routine Post-Employment Screening

Pre-employment screening is a fantastic start, but the problem with pre-employment checks is that they give you a static picture. You know about your candidate at one point in time. But people's lives change, circumstances change. And in order to truly "know" an employee, you will need to run post-employment screening, giving you an updated look at the background of someone you've hired. We'll get to the whys and wherefores in a moment, but first, what kind of screening are we talking about here?

Infinity Screening

Infinity screening means screening a person throughout his or her employment. In some cases this will be a legal necessity, in others simply a safeguard but important nevertheless. The kind of screening we're talking about here is:

- **Social Media:** Keeping updated with an employee's social media life can give you a glimpse of what is going on in their "real life" world. Candidates are more apt to post on topics that can be detrimental in an employment decision. Perhaps they exhibit violence, discrimination or a serious threat. It is critical to have a process to identify these red flags. A handle on social media accounts can mean picking up clues that you may otherwise miss about a person's employment.

- **Criminal Records:** Crime happens, and just because a candidate has a clear criminal record during pre-employment screening doesn't mean that it's going to stay that way. Knowing about ongoing cases or convictions that could affect an employee's position is key.

- **Credit Checks:** Generally used only for employees who have access to company funds or key financial positions, credit checks give you insight into an employee's financial status. Fraud, embezzlement, and simple stealing all happen, and knowing a person's credit history may provide evidence or motive for these things.

- **Healthcare Compliance:** Employees in the medical field are required to be checked out annually to ensure that no Medicare/Medicaid fraud allegations have been made, and to ensure that their licensing is up to date. The Office of the Inspector General will also list complaints made against medical professionals.

- **DMV Checks:** In some cases these are required (for employees with commercial driving licenses), but even if not required, a DMV check can be an important one to run. Knowing about driving infractions could be important if an employee drives a company car, for example, or even if they simply depend on their car to get them to work. And occasionally DMV records throw up other results, such as minor drug offenses (if marijuana is found in a vehicle during a traffic stop, for example).

You will also need to keep in mind the best practices and requirements for your particular industry. For example, commercial drivers are required by the US Department of Transportation to undergo regular random drug testing. Such requirements should obviously play a role in infinity screening.

Incident-Based Screening

As well as considering infinity screening, you'll also need to think about incident-based screening. What do you do if something happens? Incidents can and do happen in the workplace. From sexual harassment claims to stealing petty cash, threatening behavior to workplace shootings, and it's vital that you are prepared to deal with such incidents.

Obviously, you need protocols in place to deal with incidents. Knowing who does what, what the consequences are, and what your legal responsibilities are, is important. Having set procedures for likely incidents is simply good practice.

But when it comes to screening, you have another concern. Are you legally allowed to investigate an employee after an incident? Well, as long as your pre-hire consent to screening was on point, in most cases you should be clear to investigate. You want to be extremely careful around the information returned and how it is used. While an "evergreen" consent form should give you clearance to run checks on an employee at any point in time, you will, of course, need legal guidance on this, but it's good practice to ensure that any pre-hiring screening consent form also allows for post-hiring screening. Ensuring that any action taken is in accordance with the proper laws and guidelines is critical!

If your initial consent form was not evergreen, or if an incident has occurred that requires you to screen in ways not covered by your initial consent form, then you will need to acquire specific consent from the employee concerned. Again, legal advice is recommended if there's any doubt whatsoever about the checks you want to run.

Injury-Based Screening

And the same thing applies to injury-based screening. You need protocols in place to deal with what happens after a workplace injury occurs, and you need to ensure you have full consent to run any investigations necessary to resolve the issue.

But there are two more important concerns when it comes to injury-based screening. The first is that you conduct a full post-loss investigation. The idea here is to find out exactly what happened in order that you can evaluate your liabilities properly, and to try to avoid the same situation reoccurring. Plus, you will want to ensure that the employee truly is injured to the degree that they claim to be (you'd be surprised how often they are not).

Secondly, you need to determine your potential liability and ensure that you do not go beyond this. When coming to a settlement or agreement with an injured party you do not, obviously, want to spend more than you are required to.

Why Is This So Important?

So much for what you should be doing, but why should you be doing it? There are two reasons why you should be engaging in post-employment screening:

As Part of Your Risk-Mitigation Strategy

Probably the most obvious reason here is that you want to minimize your risk across the board. For much the same reasons that you want to minimize your risks when hiring, after hiring you want to ensure that the bad stuff doesn't happen, or if it does that you have minimal liability for it.

And the worst does happen. Employees steal and cheat, workplace violence happens, as does sexual harassment, accidents, injuries, and even death. By running post-employment screening, you are doing what you can to ensure that these things don't occur.

Of course, there are no guarantees, but catching that embezzlement after a month rather than after three months, finding that an employee has lost a client immediately rather than after a few weeks, and knowing that an employee isn't exhibiting signs of the injury they have claimed for, are all important. While you can't stop the bad stuff, you can minimize your legal and financial responsibilities for it. And not to overdramatize here, but with the increase in workplace violence, post-employment screening can, and does, save lives.

Because of Negligent Retention Liability

Your second concern is something called negligent retention liability. The tort of negligent retention legally requires that you maintain (where appropriate) responsibility for the consequences of an employee's action while in your employ if those actions could have reasonably been prevented.

Let's look at a brief example here. Say you have an employee who punches a customer in the face. The customer is obviously upset and injured, and wishes to take legal action against you. Surely you can't be held responsible for the actions of your employee? After all, you didn't punch the customer. But if the courts can prove that there were reasonable ways for you to suspect that the employee could be violent (perhaps he has violent convictions on his criminal record), or that the employee has acted in this way before and reasonable measures were not taken (perhaps he punched another customer and you did not take appropriate action such as firing the employee or placing him in a position away from customers), then yes, you do have responsibility for his actions.

As a consequence of negligent retention, you have a liability. And to minimize this liability you need to ensure that you are fully aware of any background issues or employment behavior that could later become an issue, and that you deal with these issues or behaviors appropriately before an incident occurs. If it ever comes down to it, post-hire screening may prove to the court that you have done your due diligence and are not at fault.

Processes and Considerations for Post-Employment Screening

You know what you should be doing and why, but what about how? There are a few processes and considerations here that you'll need to keep in mind:

1. When deciding to implement post-hiring screening, it's essential that the proper guidelines and documentations are in place to not only effectively screen employees, but also to take the appropriate action. Taking action when you are not legally permitted to will simply create more harm than good. As always, legal advice is a key part of setting up these processes, since laws do vary by state.

   As an example, let's say that your employees have all agreed to an annual DMV check. You run the check and find that one of your employees has a drug charge on their record. Your workplace rules do not require that he report that drug charge, and having such a charge does not impact his work performance (you aren't, for example, a pharmaceutical company that may have strict rules on drug records). Does the employee have the right to challenge your findings? Do you have the right to fire him or her because of the charge? This is thorny legal ground, and could be seen as discrimination. That is why you'll need to go through your attorney before making any decisions on the case.

2. Do ensure that your initial pre-hire screening consent form is an evergreen form that gives you ongoing permission to screen throughout the employment period. Doing things right the first time will save a lot of trouble down the line, and will mean that you don't need to request permission to

screen from an employee who may be irate, injured, or whom you simply don't yet want to alert to the fact that they're being screened (in the case of financial fraud perhaps).

3. Consider what you are going to do about existing employees. If you decide to implement post-hiring screening tomorrow, what will you do about the employees who are currently working and have no history of ongoing checks?

You know the risks here—the risks of holding on to a potential dangerous employee, the risks of negligent retention—so screening everyone (and not being discriminatory) is the obvious answer. There are both pros and cons, though.

On the positive side, being alert to any potential issues minimizes your risk. On the negative side, what do you do with information once you've found it? That's more of a sticky issue.

Another example: a bank has a teller who is arrested and charged with assault. The teller does not report this to his employer (and the employer does not specifically require him to). The employee pleads guilty, serves weekends in jail, and continues to do his job. In fact, if it weren't for infinity screening, the employer would never know about the assault charges and jail time at all.

So what is to be done once the charges and imprisonment are uncovered? We come back to the same issue that we had in point 1, where appropriate action is a legal minefield. The charges did not affect the employee's job performance, the charges were not specifically required to be reported, and perhaps the employee in question is a great guy who's well liked and popular. To fire or not to fire? It's a tough question, and you'll need legal advice as well as the aid of your already set-up procedures for dealing with workplace incidents.

Yes, recently implemented post-hire screening should apply to everyone, including current employees, in order to minimize your risk. But you should also consider the actions that will, can, or should be taken if negative information comes to light about a current employee.

I've been using the terms "employer" and "employee" throughout this chapter, but we mustn't forget about our alternative staffing possibilities here.

What About Subcontractors and Gig Workers?

In the case of post-hiring screening there should be no difference between employees, subcontractors, and gig workers. The risks are the same; therefore, the mitigation strategy should be the same. Subcontractors and gig workers should be subject to the same continuous screening process as employees. The only difference here will be the legal ramifications and considerations when it comes to firing. As an employer, your responsibilities are fewer when it comes to subcontractors and gig workers.

Workplace violence, shootings, injuries, compensation claims, stealing, embezzlement, and harassment all happen, and the consequences of these incidents are higher when an employer doesn't take post-hiring screening into account. Not thinking about what happens after hiring is a mistake, and one that could have vast consequences. These risks are reduced when infinity screening is used. But do remember that all investigations must be done with consent, which is why having an evergreen initial consent form is so important. You need to protect yourself not only during the hiring process, but also throughout an individual's term of employment.

We've taken a look at why and how screenings should happen, and discussed legal responsibilities and implications in brief. But as employers we are bound strictly by laws concerning what we can and cannot do when it comes to employees and other workers. So it's time now to take a more in-depth look at the weighty matter of legal implications and concerns when it comes to screening.

Chapter Five

Legal Implications and Concerns

As an employer you are bound by a variety of laws that determine what you can and cannot do. It should come as no surprise then that there are laws concerning background investigations, both pre-hire and post-hire. Before we get into these, let me first say that this chapter is in no way a replacement for legal counsel. Laws can, and do, change; and they also vary by state, meaning it's impossible to give a comprehensive rundown of every statute that you must abide by. We're going to be looking at the major issues here, but specific legal advice for your state and situation is still recommended. Having said that, let's dive into the legal implications and concerns that revolve around background investigations.

The Basics

Background investigations are governed primarily by the FCRA (the Fair Credit Reporting Act). This is the same federal act that controls credit reporting agencies. And if you think about it, this makes sense. A credit reporting agency collects data to provide a report stating whether you are eligible for credit. A background investigation collects data to provide a report stating whether you are eligible for employment. From a legal standpoint this means that background investigations are considered to be "consumer reports."

Failing to abide by the rules set down by the FCRA has civil and statutory penalties. Basically, ignore the FCRA processes and you'll find yourself in trouble. These vary from fines to huge class-action lawsuits, and rather obviously, you don't want to find yourself on the wrong side of the FCRA. This means that it's essential that you stay up to date with FCRA guidelines and follow them to the letter. There are other laws that you'll need to consider, which we'll get to later in this chapter. But the main thing you need to concern yourself with initially is following FCRA guidelines.

What Does the FCRA Require?

The FCRA is designed to protect both you as the employer, and potential employees. It regulates the accuracy, fairness, and privacy of information in all consumer reports. In this case, consumer reports are defined as "any written or oral or other communication by a CRA [consumer reporting agency] bearing on a consumer's credit worthiness, credit, credit capacity, character, reputation, personal characteristics, mode of living, as a factor in establishing consumer eligibility for credit, insurance or employment purposes."* Clearly, this includes background investigations.

Employees or potential employees are given rights and protection, and employers are given a set of rules that they must abide by. There are a few things that you need to be aware of in terms of FCRA compliance.

1. Time Frame

The FCRA has something that we refer to as the "seven-year rule." This states that with the exception of criminal convictions, any information older than seven years cannot be used in a consumer report. Things such as civil lawsuits, arrest records, and tax liens cannot be reported in a background investigation if they are older than seven years. If you base a hiring decision on such old information, you will be liable under the FCRA.

---

*   https://www.ftc.gov/enforcement/rules/rulemaking-regulatory-reform-proceedings/fair-credit-reporting-act

I just said that criminal convictions are not included in the seven-year rule, but this doesn't mean that you're free to do what you like with criminal conviction data. The FCRA does not forbid the use of such information if it's older than seven years, but many state laws do. And these depend on the state.

Just as an example, New York state law forbids the use of criminal conviction records older than seven years for use in a consumer report (or background investigation) for someone who earns less than $25,000 a year. California and Texas do not allow any reporting of convictions older than seven years.

In addition to this, some states place restrictions on reporting of non-convictions (not guilty verdicts, for example). In California non-convictions cannot be reported at all; in Maryland they can only be reported if they occurred within the last seven years.

There's an important lesson here: FCRA compliance is the legal minimum for all companies in the United States. However, state laws can, and often do, place the bar much higher. This is why it's essential to get legal advice when considering background investigations, ensuring that you comply not only with the FCRA, but also with any applicable state laws.

2. Non-Compliance

The FCRA does have penalties for failing to comply. These penalties are generally financial, with set fines of up to $2,500 per violation. However, in addition to set fines, a further amount may also be payable in the case of actual damages or emotional distress, meaning the actual cost of non-compliance may be far higher. This isn't just a question of statutory penalties, however.

Failing to comply with the FCRA can result in opening a company up to legal proceedings. Job applicants can sue employers who have failed to abide by the FCRA. In the case of companies that solicit large numbers of employees (think Wal-Mart or Target), this also opens up the threat of class-action lawsuits, with the accompanying threat of huge financial liabilities.

3. Additional Requirements

In addition to the main procedural requirements that will be listed below, there is another requirement you should be aware of. If you are gathering an "investigative report," the FCRA requires that you have a disclosure form for this specific kind of investigation (in addition to the regular disclosure forms discussed below). An investigative report includes anything where an investigator will talk to other people about an applicant. In the case of an employment background check, this would include things like talking to references or past employers. If this is part of your background investigation (and it should be!), then you must provide your potential employee with a disclosure form that states that you are going to be discussing him or her with others.

4. Procedural Requirements of the FCRA

When it comes to what you're actually required to do in terms of complying with the FCRA, there are four main processes you'll need to go through. Some of these have been discussed in earlier chapters, but I will briefly summarize them below to keep them fresh in your mind:

i. Disclosure and Pre-Authorization

Before beginning your background investigation, you must disclose to an employee or potential employee that the investigation will happen. This disclosure must be written, and must be a self-standing document (not embedded in other material). You must also obtain the employee's written authorization to allow the investigation to go forward.

ii. Pre-Adverse Action Letter / Copy of Report / Statement of Rights

Before coming to any decision about hiring (or firing) based wholly or in part on a background investigation, you must provide the employee with three things. The first of these is a letter saying that adverse action is being considered (i.e., you're thinking about not hiring the person in question). The second is a copy of the background investigation report. The third is a statement of the employee's rights under FCRA.

iii. Waiting Period

The FCRA does not specify a waiting period; however, you must wait a reasonable period between supplying the employee with the items in part ii and proceeding to part iv. At least five days is recommended. This allows the employee to become acquainted with his rights, and decide whether to challenge the background investigation or not. Mistakes do happen, and in some cases information on a background investigation report may be incorrect.

iv. Adverse Action Letter

Finally, when the waiting period has ended, you are required to send an adverse action letter telling the employee that he has not been hired (or has been fired, depending on circumstance). You are also required to provide a post–adverse communication that includes the name and contact information of the agency that performed the background investigation. This communication must include a statement that tells the employee that the agency in question did not make the hiring/firing decision, and cannot provide any further information about the hiring/firing decision. You must also include the information that the employee is entitled to receive a free copy of the full background investigation report within 60 days.

5. State Requirements

This has already been mentioned, but it's more than worth mentioning again. The FCRA only covers the federal minimum requirements for running background investigations. Individual states do have their own laws, which are often more stringent than those imposed by the FCRA. It is essential that you are versed in the employment laws of your state and how they impact background investigations!

What About the EEOC?

The EEOC, or Equal Employment Opportunity Commission, also has a role to play in avoiding legal risk when running background checks. Obviously, the EEOC protects potential employees against discrimination. It's no longer legal to advertise for only white employees, or to refuse to hire someone because she's female, or over the age of forty. Also perhaps obvious is the fact that you cannot run background checks on only certain kinds of people. If you run credit checks only on white employees but not black, or only on those under forty but not those over, you're blatantly discriminating. But the EEOC does more than this, particularly when it comes to criminal convictions.

EEOC requirements are a little less clear than those of the FCRA when it comes to criminal records. However, the essence of the EEOC's concern is that a criminal conviction not be used to discriminate. This involves two issues.

First, the same standards must be applied to everyone, regardless of age, gender, or race. Special care must be taken when dealing with issues that are a particular problem for those of a particular race, nationality, sex, or gender. This means that you cannot exclude certain criminal convictions if by doing so you disadvantage those of a particular age, race, gender, or color. This can be tough to get your head around, so let's look at a very hypothetical example. Let's say that statistically more than 60% of purple people have convictions for the serious crime of eating apples, while only 5% of green people have the same conviction. Well, if you state that you will not hire anyone with a conviction for eating apples, then you could be seen as discriminating against purple people in favor of green people.

Second, the EEOC emphasizes that should you deny employment because of a criminal conviction, that denial should be based on an individualized assessment of the candidate, rather than a blanket ban. You cannot simply say "I won't hire anyone with a conviction." You must consider the applicant in question, consider the nature of the crime he or she was convicted of, and consider how that crime/conviction pertains to the nature of the job they are applying for. For example, you may be right in denying the position of pharmaceutical tech to someone with a drug conviction. But you are on far shakier ground when denying that same applicant the position of warehouse worker, since it's unlikely that a prior drug conviction will impact his job performance in the same way.

In short, the EEOC is concerned with preventing discrimination based on any "non-changeable" factor, such as race, age, national background, disability, or gender. In order to not run afoul of the EEOC, you must ensure that you are applying all processes equally, and that you are not inadvertently discriminating by placing blanket bans on certain characteristics, qualifications, or convictions.

And the FTC?

The FTC, or Federal Trade Commission, enforces the FCRA. If you fail to comply with the FCRA, it's the FTC that will be coming after you. And to be clear, it's the companies involved that the FTC sues, not the agency that's running your background checks. The FTC does also issue guidelines that help you comply with the FCRA. Most of this information has already been covered in the FCRA section. However, there are a few additional guidelines from the FTC about creating appropriate authorization forms that are useful.

The FTC recommends that in order to stay FCRA compliant, your authorization forms adhere to these basic principles:

- They do NOT include legal jargon that claims to release you from liability for getting, running, or using a background investigation report.

- They do NOT include language that asks a prospective hire to certify that all the information on his or her application is accurate.

- They do NOT use language that asks prospective hires to acknowledge that your company's decision to hire or not hire is based on factual, non-discriminatory reasons.

- They are NOT overly broad in that they allow the release of information that the FCRA does not permit to be included in an investigation report (such as information that would break that seven-year rule).

Other Legal Trends

In addition to the above, there are several legal trends that are affecting how you employ people, and how we run background checks. We'll take into account some of the biggest of these below. But first, this seems a good point to reiterate the fact that what was above concerns federal laws. State laws can be, and are, different. In fact, even municipal laws can vary. It is absolutely essential that you educate yourself on laws for your particular location, not just laws on the federal level. Several of the legal trends we are about to discuss are matters of state, rather than federal, law. So once again, I urge you to get legal counsel before assuming that you are compliant with all relevant hiring laws.

1. Ban the Box

Ban the Box is a campaign that aims to promote fair hiring for those with criminal convictions. Their goal is to ban the "do you have a criminal conviction" box from job applications. Thus far 31 states and over 150 cities and counties have adopted this proposal. In these areas companies are NOT permitted to ask about criminal convictions on applications, though they may ask about them later in the hiring process. The idea is that companies should consider a candidate's qualifications first, rather than disregarding an application simply because an applicant has stated that he or she has a conviction. The Ban the Box initiative gives applicants a fairer chance of gaining employment. Whether or not your area is affected by Ban the Box legislation depends on where you are in the US, so again, you'll need legal advice.

2. Salary History

Another relatively new legal trend is banning questioning about salary history. A number of states and municipalities are now forbidding HR to ask about a candidate's current or past pay level in an attempt to close the pay gap based on gender or race. The idea is that by asking a candidate about their pay level you can then base your offer on their past history, which reinforces the tendency to pay women or certain racial groups lower amounts. For the most part, you are still allowed to ask about a candidate's salary expectations, or if they have any salary requirements, but in states that have legislated against salary history questions, you cannot ask specifics about actual salary in current or past jobs. Again, you'll need legal counsel to find whether your area is affected by this.

3. Use of Credit Reports

The use of credit reports in background investigations is a very sticky issue. The problem with credit reports is that they tend to paint everyone with the same brush, without taking anything into consideration. Say that I check your credit report and you have a score of 600. Well, what does that mean exactly? You were late on your car payment twice, which sounds bad. But perhaps you were in the hospital during that time (a fact that I couldn't know because a credit report doesn't give me that information). A good or bad credit report doesn't actually tell us much about an applicant, other than that they have good or bad credit. And even that might be misinformation, since credit reports are not always accurate.

Perhaps more to the point is how exactly does a person's credit score affect their ability to do a job? Well, it probably doesn't. If you're hiring for a CFO position, then a credit report might be relevant, since if a candidate is poor at managing his own finances, he's less likely to be good at managing your company's. For most other positions? Good or bad credit doesn't really have much to do with job performance.

Credit reports are discriminatory, which means that if you're not exceptionally careful to ensure that good/bad credit is key to job performance for a position, then you might find that the EEOC or FTC becomes involved in a decision not to hire. You cannot simply not hire someone for, say, a warehouse stocking job, simply because they have bad credit, since that credit doesn't have any relevance to their job performance.

There are currently no federal laws to forbid the use of credit reports in hiring, though there are city and state laws that do so. The Equal Employment for All Act of 2017 is a federal bill that has gone through Congress twice and been denied, but if it eventually passes, it will forbid credit checks for employment use on a federal level.

Unless you have a very clear and obvious reason to run a credit check (i.e., you're hiring for a heavily finance-oriented job), then running credit checks is generally not a good idea, even if your specific state or city does not forbid them. There are alternatives. A background investigation that covers bankruptcies, liens, and financial judgments should be enough to tell you relevant financial information in a non-discriminatory way, thus avoiding the credit report issue altogether.

4. Drug Testing and Marijuana

Finally, there's the issue of drug testing. For a long time, drug testing was a fairly standard part of the hiring process, with candidates who tested positive generally being excluded from the hiring pool. But as we all know, drug legalization laws are rapidly changing and this has a huge effect on drug testing for the hiring process.

Marijuana is currently legal in nine states, as well as the District of Columbia. Applicants can legally smoke marijuana in many places, and may have medical marijuana cards that allow the prescription use of the drug. Partially because of this, many companies have stopped testing for marijuana, or at least no longer drop positive-testing candidates from the hiring pool. In fact, given the tightness of the employment pool in general, some companies simply don't do drug testing, believing that they limit their choice of potential hires too much.

There is definitely a challenge involved here. How do we combine the fact that some drugs are now legal with the realities of the employment market and the risk that possible drug use can pose to the hiring company? And there is no real, easy answer to this. Partly you will need to consider the possible impact of drug use on job performance. There's an obvious difference between a warehouse stockperson who smokes marijuana and a long-haul truck driver who smokes it. And partly you'll need to evaluate the risk to the company should that employee be involved in some kind of trouble while under the influence. Again, that warehouse stockperson might, say, drop a couple of cases of goods, incurring damage and some financial loss. That long-haul truck driver, on the other hand, could kill someone in a road accident.

The issue of drug legalization and drug testing is so new that there are no clear guidelines yet on the best way to handle hiring drug screens. But the essence of the situation comes down, as it generally does, to risk, and how much risk a company is willing to take balanced against how discriminatory a non-hire for a positive drug test could be seen to be.

I do need to once again state that this chapter is no replacement for good legal advice, and counsel should be taken when setting up hiring practices, particularly when state and city laws also need to be taken into account. The legal hurdles of fair hiring can be complicated, and I've given you only the basics. But with an overview of the sort of legal concerns you're facing, perhaps now it's time to turn to something more practical: the actual policies and procedures that should be implemented.

Chapter Six

Hiring-Specific Policies and Procedures

The policies and procedures you introduce into the hiring and employment processes are key to preventing future issues. At this point, the preceding statement should be common sense. But what exactly should you be doing? In this chapter I'd like to begin to map out exactly the policies and procedures you should be considering so that you can tailor them to your own needs as a company.

The Importance of Policies and Procedures

The safety of your organization is paramount. We have discussed at length the consequences of taking risks in hiring and in employment, and the potential cost of making mistakes. Policies and procedures when properly implemented will minimize these risks and costs. However, you will need to decide how risk-averse your organization is. What is good policy for some, may not be for others. If you make pharmaceuticals, then a candidate with a drug record may not be a wise choice. But if you make furniture, for example, that same candidate may not present the same kind of risk.

So your first decision is going to be taking a look at the specific risk situation in your organization and deciding what is and isn't appropriate. You will also want to think about how you will portray this risk to stakeholders.

When deciding on policies to implement, you should consider all areas. We're talking about both physical and cyber security, as well as social and employment risks here. You need to be clear on dos and don'ts. Are outside computers to be allowed in a building? What about weapons? Are key cards necessary? How are you going to educate employees about allowing others entry into locked spaces? Will a visitor require an escort? What are your policies about use of social media and use of the company name?

Try not to be too overwhelmed—we are going to look at some of these questions in more detail, beginning with the specific policies for hiring.

Hiring-Specific Concerns

When dealing specifically with hiring, there are several policy areas you'll want to think about. Key points to consider are as follows:

- Your internal policies on whom to screen, when to screen, and at what level an employee will be screened on. Are you going to screen all candidates? Or only the top three? Are you running full background checks? At what point during the interview process will background investigations be done?

- Ensuring that all appropriate laws, both state and federal, are followed. This includes FCRA, ADA, EEOC, anti-discrimination, privacy, and other state and federal laws. Obviously, these vary a little by location, so it's essential to get proper legal advice before coming to a decision on how your hiring will be done.

- Levels of due diligence completed within the organization, keeping in mind that different positions call for different levels of due diligence.

- Not inquiring into criminal records until the appropriate time.

- Ensuring that not only is the FCRA properly followed but that applicants are appropriately informed as to their rights under

HIRING-SPECIFIC POLICIES AND PROCEDURES

FCRA (the right to challenge a background investigation report, for example).

- Ensuring that all stakeholders will be properly trained in the procedures and policies that have been decided upon.

- Ensuring that there are no departmental mix-ups. Who owns the screening process? Either HR or security must take full responsibility to ensure that no one can slip through the cracks.

- Ensuring that whoever takes responsibility for the hiring process is aware of changing laws and regulations, as well as practices inside the company. Laws and regulations do change frequently, and not keeping up with nuanced changes could impact your organization's liability. Who will be responsible for keeping track of changes in legislation? How will those changes be communicated and to whom?

These are broad brushstroke questions that you should be asking as you define the policies that are appropriate for your organization. In some cases you may need to drill down further, but at the least these are the things you'll need to take into consideration. And when it comes to selecting candidates, there are even more issues to think about.

Candidate-Selection Policy Concerns

From initial contact to hiring, the processes involved in onboarding a new employee can be very complex. Some of the below concerns we've discussed in detail in other chapters; others we've only touched upon. But below you'll find the specific issues to be considered when deciding on candidate-selection policies and procedures.

- **Recruitment and Selection of Candidates:** How will you recruit candidates for a position? Using head hunters, networking, posting ads, taking into account referrals from other employees? Are you ensuring that recruitment is anti-discriminatory and that you are best targeting the kind of candidates that are suitable for the role?

- **Application for Employment:** Are your application and process keeping with state and federal laws? Do your applications need updating? How will applications be handled and by whom?

- **Interview Process:** Will you interview in person? Over the phone? By Skype or some other internet communication? Are you ensuring that you're abiding by relevant laws during the interview process (for example, laws regarding the recording of conversations via phone, which vary by state)? How should the interview process run? Personally, we use Topgrading in my organization, but your needs may differ. You should have a clearly outlined procedure for how candidates go from applicants to employees, however.

- **Assessments:** How are you going to assess a candidate? This includes not only assessing any essential skills, but also discovery assessments, psychological assessments, Myers-Briggs personality tests, and the like. Systems like Outmatch can be highly useful in helping assess candidates. Plus, you'll need to think about when candidates will be assessed. At what point in the interview process does assessment become necessary?

- **Background Investigation Documentation:** How will you ensure that candidates get the appropriate background investigation documentation (release forms, disclosure forms)? Are those forms legally compliant?

- **Background Investigation:** We have covered this in great detail. But just to recap, you'll need to define procedures for what is done during a background investigation, when it is done, and how it is done. And you'll need to be clear on your legal obligations (taking into account things like the seven-year rule).

- **Results: Use and Interpretation:** What are you going to do with the results of a background investigation? What are your policies on, say, positive drug testing? On criminal records? What if a college degree turns out to be false? You need to consider two aspects here. First is your company's policy on background results (for example, a pharmaceutical company may see a drug charge as a definite deal-breaker). Second, you need to decide the process that continues after the results are in. If based on an investigation you're going to hire someone, what are the next steps? If based on an investigation you're not going to hire someone, what are the next steps? Remember that you must ensure the candidate knows his or her rights and is given an opportunity to challenge the investigation results. This is covered more in depth in chapter five.

- **Criminal Records:** How does a criminal record apply to the role you're trying to fill? Not only must your investigation of criminal records be done according to law (the seven-year rule, or whatever is the legislation in your state), but you must also consider whether a record has an effect on the role you're filling. A drug charge for someone applying for a warehouse job may have no impact. Someone on the sex offender registry, on the other hand, will not be suitable for a job that involves being around children.

- **Adverse Action:** What is your adverse action process? Again, this is covered in more detail in chapter five, but you do have to fulfill certain legal requirements here.

- **Legal Implications:** Your decision to hire or not hire will have legal implications (for example, opening yourself up to the risk of being sued for discrimination). Are you informed as to what these are? Are you prepared for them? Are you setting a precedent? Deciding to ignore a drug charge on one candidate's background investigation means you will potentially be expected to on the next candidate's, or risk discrimination.

- **Training:** Finally, you need to consider training. Your current staff members need to be trained in the interview and application processes in order that they not inadvertently create legal or discrimination issues. How are you going to train employees to ensure that the processes and procedures you decide upon are utilized in the way they should be?

Obviously, this is a lot to take in. And that's exactly why it's important to set up policies and procedures before beginning the hiring process, ensuring that all of these eventualities are covered. Aside from hiring- and interviewing-specific concerns, there are also a few other things you should be thinking about at this point.

Other Procedures, Policies, and Best Practices

While we will be going over actual employment processes in the next chapter, there are a few things that it's worth bearing in mind while drawing up hiring procedures. There are four real areas of concern here.

1. Onboarding

When thinking about onboarding new employees, you need to consider your organization's culture, core values, and vision, and how the employee will fit into these. A better employee fit will mean higher retention rates. And while it may not be a fantastic idea to take a far-less-qualified candidate who will be a good company fit over a highly qualified one who will not, employee fit does still need to be a consideration. Obviously, your organizational culture, core values, and vision will need to be defined in order that you may better judge how good a fit a candidate may be.

You will also need to consider other factors of bringing on a new employee. This includes potentially training him or her to do the role he or she has been hired for, as well as considering succession plans. Will the new employee work alongside a leaving or retiring employee for a certain period of time? Or will he or she walk into a cold position that has been left empty and be trained on the job?

2. Retention and Engagement

You will also need to think about how best to engage these new employees and how to keep them in their jobs. This may involve additional training or certifications, as well as tiered levels of employees.

3. Leave

You will also need to keep in mind that accidents happen, in many senses of the word. This means considering potential extra costs of a new hire, including worker's compensation (for accident and injury in the workplace), FMLA (family leave), and disability (for lasting injury). These costs will be your responsibility should something happen, and it would be negligent not to take them into account. In many cases compensation and leave will be determined by state laws, but you will also want to implement a company-wide procedure so that not only are laws adhered to, but all employees are treated equally.

4. Post-Hire Investigations

Last but not least, you will need to consider background investigations that may need to occur after hiring is already done, and there are two concerns here.

The first of these is infinity screenings. We have discussed these in an earlier chapter, but implementing processes of continual screening, whether annual or done when someone takes on a new role, can help mitigate your risk. Should you opt for infinity screenings, you will once again need to ensure that laws are abided by and that proper consent has been given, and that employees are informed that screening will form part of your company-wide policy.

Second, you will need to consider incident-based screenings. Under what circumstances may screenings happen again? If someone is taking too much time off, if money or assets go missing, if sexual harassment occurs, what are your screening procedures going to dictate? Putting the procedures into place now means less worry later.

A Successful Hire

Designing and implementing set procedures and methods for hiring and recruitment will not only make the procedure smoother and easier, but will also help safeguard against the costs of a potentially bad hire. The checklist of things to consider may seem long, but the consequences of not being thorough can be very costly indeed.

But what about once somebody is hired? What about differences between employees, gig workers, and contractors? Hiring-specific policies and procedures tell only part of the story. So let us move on to best practices for employees and get into more detail.

Chapter Seven

Best Practices: Employees

Many companies spend time, money, and effort on successfully hiring candidates. But of those companies, many do not mitigate their risks once the hiring process is done. A job offer is not the end of this process. In fact, there's a slew of other things that must be done throughout an employee's time at a company. Spending time, money, and effort hiring a candidate is all very well, but for that to be a good investment, that employee must stay with a company and be an efficient and productive worker. This is why it's important that you utilize certain best practices when dealing with employees.

Policies and Procedures

Once an employee has a job offer and has accepted that offer, there are certain policies and procedures that should be in place to ensure that the employee becomes a valuable part of your company, and that they stay that way. We can divide these policies and procedures into several categories:

Onboarding

Your initial priority should be successfully onboarding a candidate. Having procedures in place to do this will ensure a smooth transfer and a happy employee, as well as hopefully creating clear expectations and ensuring that an employee will stay with a company. So what should be done to make this process as simple and effective as possible?

- **Complete Documentation:** Many employees spend their first morning on the job filling out paperwork. As we'll see below, there's a fair amount of paper to cover. However, having someone come in beforehand to fill out documentation will avoid wasting work hours, as well as giving an employee a chance to become familiar with the company and its location before actually starting work.

- **Set Up for Success:** Ensure that an employee knows all they need to know *before* coming in for their first day. This might entail dress code, parking rules, having ID badges made, information on lunch breaks and what is and isn't an appropriate amount of time to take, as well as things like where the local lunch spots are. In essence, you want your employee to be comfortable and ready to work from the moment they walk in the door. Again, this avoids wasting time, but it also means that an employee "feels at home" in what is for most people a stressful situation.

- **Position Paper or Agreement:** Part of the documentation that should be signed is a position paper or agreement. This should clearly state what an employee is expected to do. What are his or her responsibilities? Hours of work? What is their exact job description? It would be wrong to assume that a new employee knows exactly what their job entails. And having things in writing and a signed agreement will prevent future misunderstandings or problems.

Once an employee is initially onboarded, there are other factors that come into play. These will be important not only as part of the onboarding information (when employees should be informed about the existence of the below procedures and policies), but also as part of a long-term strategy. These are things that may change over time, that may require ongoing discussions between employees and management, but that should be clear with all current and up-to-date information passed along to employees both old and new.

Your Employee Handbook

The first of these factors is your employee handbook. Most companies have these, and many are extremely long. Length is necessary, of course, to cover all bases, but it can make the information difficult to digest.

Your first concern should be whether the handbook is up to date. In today's world, laws change frequently, even weekly, and your handbook should be updated to reflect any changes. This is especially true concerning sexual harassment law changes in the current climate, but applies to any change in legislation that affects employment. Your employee handbook should be regularly updated to reflect the most recent changes.

Second, you must be sure that the new employees in particular have had time to go over the information included in the company handbook. The best way of doing this, in my opinion, is to set aside a couple of hours to review some of the more important points with a new employee. Also, of course, you must ensure that old employees are informed of any changes to the handbook.

Finally, you must ensure that the information contained in the employee handbook is accepted by new hires. It should be clear that these are rules the employee is expected to abide by and that failing to do so can result in consequences.

Career Planning

The truth of the matter is that an employee is more likely to stay with a company when they can foresee growth in their position. A discussion about career planning not just at the beginning of an employee's tenure but also at intervals during their career can ensure that employees know the opportunities available to them.

Initially, an employee should know why they were hired. But you as a manager should know what kind of career path the employee intends to take. An employee should be informed about promotion or advancement possibilities, and the potential to apply for senior or management positions after a certain amount of time or after achieving certain goals or certifications.

Failure to have regular discussions on this topic could mean that after a year or two, an employee defects to a competitor where they are offered a more advanced position—meaning all that time, money, and effort you spent on hiring that employee have not had time to pay off.

Culture, Core Values, and Mission

It should be clear to all employees, new or not, what a company's culture, core values, and mission are. Understanding company culture is an important part of the onboarding process. Knowing that you are a casual or formal company, for example, or knowing that on Fridays everyone goes out after work for a couple of hours. In order to be a good fit, a new employee must understand the company culture and know what is expected of them in order to fit in.

But an employee must also know what the mission of a company is. What are you all there to do? How do your employees fit into this? In order for them to fulfill this mission, it must first be laid out for them.

As for core values, I have found it best to couch this in terms of success. In my business, my company's core values are integrity and a passion for excellence. I inform new employees that people who are successful in my company show a positive attitude, believe in integrity first, are successfully engaged, and show a passion for excellence. This gets across the message that not only are these the core values for my business, but that in order to be a successful employee these are the things you will need to demonstrate.

Finally, what does your company allow or not allow? Will your company live by its core values? Will it be a fire-able offense not to live by these values? Again, all these things need to be communicated to employees in a clear and concise manner.

Company Policies and Disciplinary Processes

Lastly in this section, there's the question of policies and discipline. We will circle back to disciplinary processes in more detail later in this chapter. But for now, understand that employees must know what policies exist and how they are enforced.

Policies on all aspects of code of conduct should be covered. Everything from how long a lunch break can be, to whether employees can take smoke breaks, wear jeans in the office, or have their personal cell phones with them. You should also include the basics of information security and data security, a section on what is considered theft and what the consequences will be (something that sounds intuitive but may not be, for example: would taking home a notepad from a stationery cupboard be considered theft?). Essentially, you're looking to foresee every possible action and state whether it is acceptable or not, and if not, what the consequences of such an action would be, whether that's firing or just a verbal warning.

One particular thing you may want to focus on is data breaches and violations and how this impacts the organization. With many employees nowadays having passwords to company accounts and even company laptops and computers, it's essential that employees know what is and is not acceptable, and what the potential impact of data breaches can be on an organization. With the new GDPR rules, protection of personal information is key, so employees must know how such information is protected and how they can safeguard any information that's in their possession.

Where Do Background Investigations Come In?

One of the processes you will need to implement if you haven't already is that of ongoing background investigations. We have discussed infinity screening in chapter four in detail, but I'll go over the basics here again.

There should be a process in place to screen existing employees after hiring (and a signed agreement allowing this to happen, as mentioned in chapter four). Background screening before hiring is important, but it is not enough. Life happens. Financial problems rear their heads, substance abuse becomes an issue, convictions for crimes can go unnoticed—mitigating the risk from all of these is critical to an organization. And this means infinity screening, a continuous process of ensuring that an employee is still the same "safe" employee you originally screened and hired.

Being aware of an employee's presence on social media should form a part of this infinity screening. What are potential red flags on social media that could indicate an upcoming incident? What could be done to prevent that incident? What are your processes for discovering that, say, an employee on sick leave has posted pictures from the beach? Or that an employee has posted a racist or politically inflammatory status on his or her social media? These are all questions that a responsible organization, one focused on mitigating risk, should be considering. These questions focus on what to do if an incident happens and whether awareness can prevent an incident from occurring in the first place.

Employee screening should form an important part of your regular activities for all employees in a company, and a big part of that should be being aware of what is happening on social media.

Disciplinary Processes

Disciplinary processes are an unfortunate necessity. It is important that you are very clear on what is and is not acceptable in the workplace and what the consequences of undesirable actions will be. The rules will vary, obviously, depending on your business. While for some, taking an extra ten minutes at lunchtime could be fine, for others, that could be a fire-able offense. Do not only consider rule breaking, but also think about employees who may not be performing as well as they should, or who are not fulfilling their agreed-upon role. The key thing is to be sure that you have a clear process for what happens.

What is tolerable for your workplace will depend on your circumstances, but there are various forms of corrective action that organizations employ. These include:

- Verbal warnings
- Written warnings
- Action to improve performance such as PIP (performance improvement plan) or AMP (achieving maximum performance) that are designed to help employees improve their situation
- Forced resignation
- Firing

While considering what is a punishable offense and what the consequences should be, keep in mind the potentially serious consequences for the company of disciplining or firing an employee. Obviously there's the question of a loss of investment (the time, money, and energy you spent on hiring and training an employee), as well as potential compensation (severance, legal fees and settlements in unfair dismissal cases), and also the threat of repercussions such as violence or theft on the part of departing employees. This means you do need a defined process for termination.

Termination of Employment

Employment can be terminated by either the employer or the employee. The decision to sever the employment contract is not an easy one, but once it has been made, there should be a protocol for what happens. There are several factors you'll need to take into account when designing a termination-of-employment protocol:

- What is your process for employees resigning? Is a resigning employee expected to stay on site for a certain amount of time (a notice period)?

- In the case of firing, is there a "good" time for this to happen (perhaps at the end of a financial quarter, or during a customarily quiet business period)?

- How will you deal with the handover of equipment, keys, tools, and ID cards or access cards to the site?

- How will the job transfer occur? Will the leaving employee need to train a new person to do their job? Who will take on the duties of the leaving employee?

- Will your company offer severance pay? If so, under what circumstances? For example, you may offer severance only in the case that you are downsizing, or only for certain roles.

- Will you contest unemployment?

- What about letters of reference? Will you provide them? If so, under what circumstances? Perhaps you may give letters of reference to those who have reached a certain goal, or only those who resign, rather than those who are fired.

- What will you tell other employers if they call following the leaving employee listing you as a reference on their CV?

- What will you tell the rest of the staff? Are staff to be told about the circumstances of a firing or resignation, or simply informed that it has occurred?

Alongside all of these considerations, there is also the question of safety and security. In the case of an unpleasant termination, you must ensure that you, your employees, your location, and your assets are all protected. In order to do this, you must consider the following:

- What steps exist to ensure that the employee does not return? For example, you may need to revoke their access codes, cards, or passwords. You may need to inform reception staff or security that this person is no longer allowed on site.

- Has the employee in question been informed that they are not to come back, regardless of the circumstances of their termination? Again, this may seem like common sense, but it is important to be direct and clear on this matter in case of later repercussions.

- What is the plan should the terminated employee be seen again on site? Security staff in particular may need to be informed of this. But in some cases you may wish to inform all staff that if X is seen on site then they must report this to security, or even call the police.

Best Practices: The Bottom Line

The best business practice is to ensure that your protocols and processes are clear and defined from the beginning. Everyone must understand expectations and potential issues from the moment of hiring. In order to keep employees you value, as well as to successfully rid your organization of those you do not value, you must have processes in place. Simply hiring great talent is not enough; you must also guide that talent into becoming a valuable member of your organization.

In this chapter we dealt with best practices specifically geared toward employees. But there is still the question of gig workers and contractors, so it is there that we will turn next.

Chapter Eight

Best Practices: Gig Workers and Contractors

If you are reading this book straight through, then you will probably find that this chapter is vaguely familiar. There are many similarities between best practices for employees and those for gig workers and contractors. However, there are also some important differences. And I have chosen to be thorough, despite the fact that this may mean repeating some things, for those who are using this book as a reference guide and wish to be able to pick up and read only the chapters they feel pertain to them.

Simply hiring a great candidate is not enough, whether that be an employee, gig worker, or contractor. Spending time, energy, and money on hiring is fantastic, but in order to protect the investment you have made, you must also ensure that you employ best business practices to keep that worker with your company, or, indeed, to be able to rid yourself of a worker who isn't as good as you imagined.

Policies and Procedures

Once you have decided upon a contractor or gig worker you want to work with, you will need a contract or agreement in order to proceed. This agreement will depend heavily on what the role is to be fulfilled, but do not think that just because someone is a gig worker they do not need to sign any paperwork. Getting that initial contract or agreement is essential in order to protect yourself. It should outline clearly the responsibilities of the worker or vendor company, the time frame in question, your expectations, and compensation. Once this is agreed upon and signed, then you can move forward in working with the person or company decided upon.

Onboarding

Despite the fact that we are no longer talking about employees, onboarding is still an important process. Whether they're working from home or coming into the office, whether we're talking about a gig worker or a vendor that will send contractors to you, onboarding is a vital process. Again, we're talking about expectations.

You must ensure that workers know what to expect before their first day of work. In the case of people coming into your office, that might include all the things you discuss with employees: lunch breaks, appropriate dress, lunch spots, working times. For those not coming to your location, this could include when they will be expected to be available, or contact information for those with whom they will be working. In short, you need to inform workers of all they need to make their first day on the job as successful as possible. This avoids wasting work time and ensures that cooperation goes smoothly.

Whether this is a short-term gig or a long-term contract, a solid onboarding process will be key to efficiency as well as satisfied workers. There should be no opportunity for a worker to make the excuse "But I didn't know." That applies to the small things (lunch breaks are only forty-five minutes, all papers are to be shredded, cell phones are not allowed) as well as the big things (we're located here, dress code is formal). And don't forget to arrange access to your location for those who need it, including passcodes, ID badges, or simply informing security or reception staff that new people will be on site.

Your Gig Handbook

While many organizations have an employee handbook, gig handbooks are less common. But in a changing world, where gig workers and subcontractors are becoming more common, a gig handbook (a gig or contract worker's equivalent to an employee handbook) is a necessity. In essence, a gig handbook will tell a worker everything he or she needs to know about the company and his or her role in it.

As well as obvious things that need to be covered (dress code, disciplinary action, all the things that are covered in a traditional employee handbook that gig workers should know about) there are several things that need to be made clear in a gig handbook that apply to workers whether they're on site or not:

- **Expectations:** What is expected of a worker in terms of their role. This can include hours worked, availability times, dress codes, and anything else you will expect a worker to do or be.

- **Performance:** What are you expecting from a worker in terms of work? What tasks are they to fulfill? What goals are set? Generally this is handled in the worker contract, but there is no harm in restating it.

Just as with an employee handbook, you will need to ensure that your gig handbook is up to date and reflects the most recent changes in laws or legislation in your state, particularly regarding things like the current rapidly changing sexual harassment laws.

Clarity in Position

Here is something that is unique to gig and contract workers. You must be exceptionally clear on role and requirements. Just because someone is listed as a contract worker does not actually make them one. As we discussed in earlier chapters, the definition of a contract worker is fuzzy and varies by state. You must ensure that you are clearly stating obligations that apply to gig workers only.

Schedule, compensation, and challenges should all be addressed. You want to avoid a situation where a gig worker could "accidentally" become an employee (for example, working a set number of hours, being told specifically what to do by one person, whatever the requirement is for being an employee in your state).

Failing to do this could result in the employer being penalized, or the worker suing to be compensated as an employee. You'll find a more in-depth explanation of the problems of defining gig workers vs. employees in chapter one. But be sure you are clear in your procedures that you are dealing with a gig worker and abiding by the appropriate definition of this in terms of your state laws.

Term Lengths

You will also want to specify the duration of your cooperation. In the case of a short-term gig, that time frame should be clearly defined by date. In the case of a long-term gig, you may want to consider the advantages and disadvantages of hiring someone full time for the role (or the potential of making a gig worker a full-time employee later), and whether it's better or cheaper to have a consultant for the role. This will depend on your needs, but there are pros and cons to each. A gig worker may be cheaper, for example, but a full-time employee is better bound to the company (they cannot just leave when they feel like it) and may be better informed as to their tasks simply because they work only on those tasks, as opposed to splitting their time between different gigs.

Culture, Core Values, and Mission

Just as with employees, it's important that gig workers and contractors are informed as to an organization's culture, core values, and mission. Everyone in an organization should be living the same values and culture.

In terms of culture, what kind of company are you? Formal? Casual? Do we use first names, do we wear jeans in the office? Do we spend time together outside of the office? Including gig workers and contractors into this culture will ensure not only that they're a good fit but also that they feel welcome and a part of an organization, decreasing the chances that they will choose to leave your employ early.

Similarly, what is your company's mission? What do you do? What are you hoping to achieve? How does the gig worker or contractor play a role in this? Laying out a worker's role in the company as a whole not only makes a worker happier and more efficient, but also keeps them goal oriented.

Finally, what are your core values as a company? Those things that you want your company to convey. Perhaps you value creativity, perhaps order, perhaps you strive for excellence, or for great teamwork. How does your organization demonstrate these core values? What do these values allow (or not allow for)? Perhaps, for example, you value success; therefore, taking home company equipment in order to work further in the evenings is acceptable. Perhaps you value employee satisfaction and you forbid taking work home so that employees may have better work-life balance. How does your organization live by its core values, and will not living by them be a fire-able offense?

Company Policies and Disciplinary Processes

We will go into more depth on disciplinary processes later in this chapter. However, it is important that all policies and discipline processes are clearly laid out and understood by workers. What are your policies and how are they enforced?

You will need to include all aspects of code and conduct, from the basics like dress code to information security, data security, theft, and more. Basically, you want a handbook for how you expect a worker to behave and clear repercussions for failing to meet those standards.

Pay particular attention to data and data security. With many gig workers and contractors having passwords, passcodes, company equipment, and access to data (even a telecommuting connection to sensitive company information), you must be clear on what is and is not allowable practice with this data. Data breaches cost companies millions, not just directly, but also through loss of good will and trust. All workers must know how they can treat sensitive data and what they may and may not do with it. For example, you may state that company laptops cannot be out of sight when they're outside of the building, or that data may not be copied for any reason. The advent of GDPR means that how we treat personal data is becoming a huge priority for companies.

Where Do Background Investigations Come In?

Running background investigations before hiring is common practice nowadays. However, running post-engagement checks is less common, which dramatically heightens your risk. People change, and circumstances change. A candidate who passed an initial background investigation may, for example, develop financial problems, or substance abuse problems, or get a conviction or two. If you are not doing post-hiring background investigations, you will know about none of these things.

We discussed infinity screening way back in chapter four, so I'll only touch on it briefly here. In order to mitigate risk to your organization, you should be running regular investigations into existing employees and workers. This is just as true for gig workers and contractors as it is for employees. The one difference is that some contracting companies will run their own background investigations before sending workers to your site. I would urge caution even here, however, unless you know in detail how those contractors screen, how regularly they do so, and whether their screening process is legal. See chapter four for more detail on infinity screening.

One thing you should pay particular attention to is social media. A social media presence is almost ubiquitous nowadays, and following your employees' social media accounts can form a solid part of your screening process. Here, as with other areas, you'll need a plan in place for when incidents happen. What are your protocols if you find that a worker has posted inflammatory, sexist, racist, or political statements on their social media? What are your protocols if a worker who has claimed to be ill or unable to meet a deadline posts pictures showing themselves obviously on vacation? What are potential red flags on social media that could indicate an upcoming incident? Say, a statement from a worker maligning the company and threatening violence, or leaking of data?

If social media presence is something you decide is important to your organization, then you will need protocols for dealing with incidents that can arise from the social media accounts of your workers. It's simply the responsible thing to do. You aim to respond to incidents as quickly as possible, and hopefully to spot red flags and head an incident off before it even happens. This comes down to awareness and covering all your bases. Neglect following up on employees' social media accounts at your own risk.

Disciplinary Processes

All organizations need disciplinary processes and termination protocols, whether you're dealing with employees or gig workers. The major difference here is that with gig workers and contractors you have far more leeway. While employees are strongly protected by employment laws, gig workers and contractors aren't, meaning you have more options. You do still have the same disciplinary options as you would with an employee, meaning that if there's an incident and you do not wish to fire a worker, you can still employ the following methods:

- Verbal warnings
- Written warnings
- Action to improve performance such as PIP (performance improvement plan) or AMP (achieving maximum performance) that are designed to help employees improve their situation
- Forced resignation

The difference is that should you decide on termination of the worker, then you have far more freedom and fewer concerns.

Termination of Gig Workers

You are free to terminate a contract with a gig worker or contractor whenever you feel like it, without a notice period. You may also choose to launch legal action against a worker for not fulfilling their role in a contract. This makes terminating a gig worker far easier than terminating an employee. However, it is still important to have protocols. You must decide what actions are tolerable in your organization and which aren't, and be sure to clearly outline these in your gig worker handbook or onboarding contract. You should also be sure to outline your termination protocols in your initial agreement with a gig worker. Once you have made it clear that certain actions are intolerable and how termination proceeds in your company, then there are a couple of other considerations:

- What are your protocols for return of company assets? Gig workers may have company equipment, ID cards, tools, keys, passcodes, or data. How will you go about ensuring these are returned, and what is the deadline for returning things? What will you do if items are not returned?

- Severance pay and unemployment are not concerns with gig workers; however, you may wish to consider how and when legal actions will be launched in the case of gig workers not fulfilling their contracts.

- Who will take over the role of the gig worker if they are terminated? Is there someone on site who can do so, or will you need to recruit another gig worker? If you're recruiting, who will perform the worker's role in the meantime?

- If the worker asks for a reference, will you give it to them? What will you say if another employer calls and requests information about the worker because you have been listed on a CV as a reference?

- How and when will you inform other staff of the gig worker's termination or leaving? What will they be told?

In addition to these concerns you will also need to think about safety and security. Termination is an emotional event, and one that can provoke a violent reaction. In order to mitigate risk here, you will need to think about protocols concerning:

- What steps exist to ensure that the gig worker does not return to your location (where appropriate)? Has access to buildings, databases, and servers been restricted? Do security or reception staff need to be notified that a person is no longer welcome on site?

- Has it been made clear to a worker that they are no longer to be on site, regardless of circumstances?

- What is the plan should a terminated worker be on site? Have staff members been informed? Should security be called, or should the police be called?

Best Practices: The Bottom Line

Employing gig workers and contractors is quite different from hiring regular employees, though there is a lot of crossover when it comes to post-hiring protocols. You need to protect yourself and your organization. This means having clear and defined protocols and processes that deal with risk mitigation during the employment period, not just before it. In order to be efficient, have satisfied workers, and be able to easily let go of workers you no longer wish to work with, you must have clear directives on what is and is not allowable, and what the consequences of non-allowable actions are. Screening does not stop when an initial contract is signed; constant awareness of changing situations is necessary to mitigate your risks as an organization.

We have now dealt with the generalities of post-hiring, the best business practices for working with both employees and gig workers. But what about more challenging situations? In the next chapter we will discuss some of the more difficult post-hiring challenges, along with protocols and other methods of dealing with them.

Chapter Nine
Post-Hire Challenges

As we've discussed in the last couple of chapters, the game isn't over once an employee is hired. Hiring-specific challenges are only the first hurdle when it comes to mitigating your risk as an employer. In fact, reducing risk during employment may be even more of a challenge. There are really two main scenarios here: issues arising directly post-employment, and those arising during the course of employment. Obviously, it's essential that you are able to meet the challenges of risk mitigation of your workforce, so that's what I'll be addressing in this chapter.

Direct Post-Employment Challenges

The first set of issues we'll touch upon are those that can arise immediately following employment. Throughout the course of this book, we've discussed background screening and following best practices to get the best person hired for a job. But—and here's the kicker—we're all fallible. While background investigations are an excellent way of screening candidates, they can and do miss things. This may be due to not following best practices, or to inefficiency, to incapability or simple oversight. The truth is, though, mistakes can happen in a background check.

The most common issue we see here is when an employee passes a background check, only for something to come to light after being hired. In my own experience from talking with clients, one of the common issues that arises is when an employee has passed a background investigation and been hired, only for a co-worker to feel something was not right and turn up a criminal record by running a simple Google search. Thankfully, this isn't something that happens often, but it does happen. I'll say it again: background checks are not infallible (although they are necessary). So what do you do if something arises that didn't show up on a check?

- **Conduct an Investigation:** Your first step should be to investigate for yourself what has happened. This may involve a cursory or in-depth process to uncover the truth. This often includes but is not limited to discussing the incident with the employee in question, or checking out an anonymous claim made against someone. You want all the facts at your fingertips before proceeding.

- **Assess the Outcome:** What are the repercussions of the incident? Does this new information affect the status of the employee? Or perhaps the information has no bearing on the person's job? This will depend on the nature of your business, what your risk tolerance is, and the nature of the information you have discovered.

- **Determine Course of Action:** Third, you need to decide what the consequences of this are. The employee has already been hired; do you have legal grounds to terminate him or her? (We'll discuss this a little more below.) Perhaps the incident is not something that would cause you to let an employee go, in which case do you recommend counseling (in the case of drug problems, for example), or a change in role in the company, or simply do nothing? Depending on the results of your investigation, you have several options available to you.

In the case of wanting to terminate an employee, you will need to keep in mind your legal right to terminate. And you could be on shaky ground here. In the example I mentioned above, a violent felony charge was anonymously reported concerning an employee. However, that employee had not been asked in interview or on his application if he had felonies (due to the recent trend and laws preventing employers from asking that question). It was a matter of the background investigation not finding this information. In this case, legally terminating the employee could present difficulties, since he hadn't lied, and legal advice was necessary.

Course-of-Employment Challenges

Far more common than direct post-hire challenges are those that occur during the course of employment. These challenges are myriad, but as an example may fall under one of the following headings:

- The employee commits a crime while employed.
- The employee falls on hard times, thus making financial positions higher risk than originally planned for.
- The employee has an accident, representing a financial loss to the company and perhaps the threat of legal proceedings.
- The employee does something to the employer (perhaps embezzling, or presenting threatening behavior).
- Disciplinary issues arise (perhaps the employee being consistently late).
- Performance issues arise (with the employee unable to fill his current role).
- The employee may be enticed to infiltrate the organization by outsiders in order to seek monetary gain.

And that's only a sample. Life happens; circumstances change; the level of risk presented by an employee is not constant. Because of this, you cannot rely solely on that initial pre-hiring background check to ensure your company's reputation, finances, and safety remain secure. So what can you do? When thinking about course-of-employment challenges, the most important thing you can do is to establish protocols for what to do, why, and when.

Establishing Protocols

As mentioned in the previous chapters, establishing protocols for dealing with potential challenges before those challenges arise is key. In the preceding two chapters we discussed what kind of general protocols you should have for dealing with post-hire issues with employees and gig workers/contractors. Ideally, you should be equipped to handle any issue that arises with a clear company protocol that the employee him- or herself is also aware of. There are three main areas that we need to think about when establishing protocols.

Infinity Screening

We have discussed infinity screening at length, but it's worth mentioning again here. You should run periodic screening of all employees, not just job candidates. Your screening should be done following the appropriate FCRA guidelines, and you should ensure that employees have signed an evergreen document that allows for such continuous screening to happen.

You will want to routinely check on employees throughout the course of employment by running various forms of screening, such as criminal record checks, DMV checks, and perhaps drug testing. The exact nature of which forms of screening you should use will depend on your area of business and the risks it presents (you can find more information on the kinds of checks I recommend for certain industries in chapter eleven).

You will also want to consider an employee's social media presence. Social media screening is a relatively new area in the industry, but one with growing importance because not all folks with bad intentions or bad behavior are detected by standard means (criminal DMV). When screening social media, there are four real areas of interest:

- Racist, sexist, or discriminatory behavior. Posts or pictures representing such behavior should raise red flags and urge caution when further screening an employee.

- Potential illegal behavior. Posts or pictures referencing illegal drugs, for example, or crime, should obviously raise red flags.

- Sexually explicit material. Whether this refers to adult activity or potential activity with minors, sexually explicit posts or pictures should raise those red flags.

- Threats or acts of violence. And, obviously, references to violent behavior or to threatening behavior should also raise flags.

While infinity screening should help raise awareness of new issues in an employee's history, you also need to consider more isolated cases, which we refer to as situation-based investigations.

Situation-Based Investigations

Regardless of infinity screening, incidents can and do happen. Perhaps that's a sexual harassment claim, perhaps an accident in the workplace, or an incident of violent behavior. It's essential that you have protocols in place to determine what happens after any one of a number of situations. This will require that you conduct an investigation based on the incident itself to determine exactly what transpired. It may also require legal advice as to what is and is not allowed in terms of both the incident itself and your response. Once you have determined what happened, you must then decide on an appropriate course of action.

Again, your course of action will depend on the incident and your risk tolerance as well as on what you're legally obligated to do or forbidden from doing. You might want to consider offering counseling to those with drug or violent incidents, for example. Perhaps an employee needs a change in role in order to better perform in your company. Or maybe you need to consider termination, which is our next concern.

Decisions to Terminate Employment

Finally, you must consider your practices when terminating employment. Employees have rights, and employers are not allowed to hire and fire at will anymore. This is a good thing, but it does mean you need to ensure that any termination is done rightfully. You may require legal advice before terminating an employee. You must ensure that any legal obligations in regards to severance pay, compensation, notice periods, and the like are met. These obligations will depend on your state laws, as well as on the incident that has provoked termination, so I cannot give you more specific advice than this. But do always make sure that you're in the right when terminating a contract to avoid being sued for wrongful termination later.

Post-Hire Challenges in Summary

Risk mitigation is an ongoing process, one that does not stop once an employee is hired. But by being aware, running infinity screening, and establishing protocols to deal with specific kinds of incidents, you can be assured that you are lowering your risk as much as possible.

Ongoing screening is perhaps the most valuable recommendation that I can make. Many of the calls I receive concern problems with those who have already been employed. Just as one example, I received a call about an employee who had been convicted of a crime and was serving weekends in jail. The employer had no idea, since the employee was present and correct at work on Monday morning after his weekend in jail. It was only when a colleague reported the situation that the employer realized there was a potential risk that he'd heard nothing about.

Of course, a large part of all your protocols to mitigate risk is staying within the law. Your legal rights to screen, employ, not employ, and terminate employment are strictly bound by law. Nobody wants to get sued, which is why next we're turning to avoiding litigation.

Chapter Ten

Avoiding Litigation

Litigation has been an ongoing issue against employers who wrongfully make adverse hiring decisions, or make decisions that result in harm or threats to others. Having cases brought against you as an employer or a company reflects not just on your company finances, but also on your reputation, and can cost millions in compensation and lost business. Avoiding litigation must be at the forefront of your mind when hiring (and firing).

Litigation: Example Cases

Hiring litigation has impacted many organizations around the world, from a branding and reputation perspective as well as the perspective of overall compliance. Litigation claims have arisen as a result of failure to follow FCRA guidelines, failure to follow proper screening practices, and in many cases by being discriminatory in the due diligence process. Before we get to the hows of avoiding litigation, first let's look at some example cases that serve as cautionary tales as well as helping us extract useful lessons from others' mistakes.

1. The Target Case

In April 2018, retail giant Target paid $3.7 million after being accused of racial disparity in their hiring processes. Their improper use of criminal background checks was found to unfairly affect blacks and Latinos, leading to a class action suit and a big payout. Target was not following the appropriate FCRA guidelines on using criminal background checks and suffered because of it. The proposed settlement of this case (which currently still requires court approval) calls for priority employment for eligible Latinos and blacks who applied for positions at Target after May 11, 2006, and were then denied employment because of criminal background checks; alternatively, the same group may seek a payout of up to $1000. The settlement also calls for a review of Target's background check policies by experts to determine where changes need to be made. Target has not admitted to wrongdoing.

2. The U.S. Census Bureau

In 2016, the U.S. Census Bureau was at the heart of a similar case to the above, with a class action lawsuit resulting in a $15 million payout after courts found that hiring practices unfairly discriminated against blacks and Latinos. Again, the use of criminal background checks was blamed. As well as discriminating against ethnic groups that tended to have higher rates of criminal convictions, in this case criminal background checks were also found to provide false or mistaken information.

3. The Frito Lay Case

Early in 2018, snack food company Frito Lay was forced to pay $2.4 million after courts found they improperly used disclosure forms. Under FCRA rules, a company cannot access a full background check on a job candidate without providing that candidate with "clear and conspicuous disclosure" using a form that consists solely of that disclosure. Frito Lay failed to do this and therefore violated FCRA regulations.

These are just three of a plethora of cases that have taken places across the U.S. and the world featuring companies failing to take into account best practices upon hiring. What lessons do we take away from these cases?

- Being educated in FCRA regulations and following them to the letter is key.

- Having appropriate legal paperwork to obtain permission for screening is essential.

- Running a background check is not enough. Once information is obtained, it must be studied for accuracy and for relevance to the job position.

- All efforts must be taken to ensure that discrimination (by race, sex, or anything else) does not occur when using information obtained through background screening.

- Courts can and do side with plaintiffs, in matters of fair hiring, for mistakes such as not checking that information is accurate or seemingly small infractions such as not having an independent consent form for screening.

- There are other types of litigation, including those resulting from workplace violence incidents, which can be avoided by effective practices as well.

Why This Happens

The above cases should make it quite clear that litigation happens as a result of companies failing to properly audit their existing processes to ensure that they are meeting the necessary (and often changing) legal and due-diligence-based requirements. Like it or not, there are a vast array of legal requirements that companies must meet when running both hiring and infinity screening, as well as laws determining how information gained can be used. Failing to follow these laws, and failing to stay up to date with changes in laws, can be extremely costly. Ignorance is no excuse—it is your responsibility to ensure that your processes reflect the most recent changes to laws and legislation.

What Can Be Done Differently?

In order to avoid litigation, therefore, you must ensure that your hiring and screening policies are both legal and up to date. There are things you can do to protect yourself in this area. There are three major concerns you'll need to consider.

1. An Annual Audit of Current Processes

Your hiring and screening policies should be reviewed annually at the very least. This time should be used to ensure that processes are up to date and reflect any recent changes in law. You should also use this opportunity to consider whether all parts of the process are necessary, as well as whether more stages/steps/paperwork should be added. The goal is a consistent, legal, non-discriminatory hiring process that protects the candidates as well as your company.

2. Following Best Practices

You should also ensure that you're following best practices in your hiring process. We have discussed what these are in earlier chapters (chapter two in particular goes into detail about the legalities of the hiring process), but I will recap them here briefly. Do remember that practices and laws are constantly changing and vary by location, so this is not an exhaustive list of everything that must be done; rather, it is a reminder of areas that need to be investigated and considered as part of your hiring process.

- **Application**: It is important to ensure that applications do not ask questions that are forbidden (such as the "ban the box" questions and salary history), as well as those that are non-discriminatory and abide by FCRA guidelines.

- **Release Form:** Ensure that they are signed and that they allow you to do what you need to do. Remember that FCRA laws state that a release form for a background check must be self-standing and not a part of any other paperwork. Also consider the signing of evergreen release forms that allow for infinity screening should a candidate become an employee.

- **Disclosures:** Candidates must be given the appropriate disclosure(s) by state as well as federal guidelines. This means they are informed that a background check is going to be done, and they are informed of their rights regarding this check. They should be given a copy of their FCRA Summary of Rights and be given the opportunity to obtain a copy of the resulting report themselves.

- **Due Diligence/Investigation:** Not all states allow the collection of all kinds of information. You must ensure that you are receiving not just the kinds of information you need to make a good hiring decision, but also information you are legally allowed to request. This is particularly true when it comes to criminal records, since court records and jurisdictions vary widely on what is accessible and permissible to disclose on a background check. Once you have this information, you should consider how it may or may not affect potential job performance, being careful not to be discriminatory in your use of such information.

- **Adverse-Action Process:** Again, the decision to use information found during a screening must be made legally. All attempts must be made to avoid possible discrimination, and the appropriate FCRA guidelines must be followed. The requirement involves sending a Pre–Adverse Action Notice (along with copy of the background investigation report and appropriate rights) giving the applicant ample time to review any incorrect information. Once that time period has elapsed and the applicant fails to refute the information, an Adverse Action Notice is sent advising the candidate that an official decision has been made to not hire the candidate.

- **Hiring Decisions:** If a decision is made to hire, there's a resulting flood of further responsibilities. These include contracts, work site agreements, employee handbooks, clear outlining of a role, potential future with a company, infinity screening disclosure, and plenty more. Earlier chapters cover this in greater detail, but these practices should also come under examination when you are doing your annual audit of your hiring processes.

- **Privacy: GDPR is now a requirement for how businesses process and handle data but not just limited to the UK.** Does your organization handle data? Beware. GDPR will set the standard for the rest of the world on data privacy and management. As an employer, you are maintaining personal information, and it is critical to ensure that protocols are in place to protect that.

3. HR Compliance

Finally, you must, must, *must* ensure that everything you do is compliant with relevant HR laws. This involves staying up to date with the latest trends in human resources as well as following any changes in state or federal laws. I cannot emphasize enough just how often these laws change, making running afoul of them all the easier.

Chapter five goes into detail about some of the more recent trends in HR. As a recap, here are some of the things that are in a state of flux at the time of writing:

- **Ban the Box:** A movement to ban the "Do you have any criminal convictions?" question from job applications. In some states this has already become law and is rapidly becoming accepted practice in many other areas.
- **Salary History:** A movement toward not asking about prior salaries in an attempt to close the gender and race pay gap. It is illegal to ask about salary history in some states now.
- **Credit Reports:** A movement to ban the use of credit reports in making hiring decisions. Basically the idea behind this is that for most positions a person's credit history has no impact on their job performance. As of right now using credit reports is not banned, but legislation is currently being considered, and the practice is a tricky one that could easily result in an unfair dismissal claim.
- **Drug Testing:** A movement toward not testing for drugs. As marijuana becomes legal in more and more areas, many

companies are moving away from drug testing employees unless the role they are to fulfill (driving, being around children, being around pharmaceuticals) could be negatively impacted by drug use.

With such rapidly changing trends and laws, staying up to date is essential. And as always, getting good legal counsel on the validity and legality of your hiring processes is key. Instituting solid processes for hiring and screening is important, but doing so only once is not enough. Hiring processes should be constantly evolving in order to reflect changes in laws and trends. By auditing your processes and ensuring that everything is up to scratch, you will be doing the most you can to avoid future legislation.

We have discussed a lot of information in the preceding chapters, so moving forward I'd like to collate some of the data into something more practical. Best practices vary by location and by industry. Having a checklist of the type of practices we recommend by industry should help you get started in designing your own hiring processes, which is where we turn to next.

Chapter Eleven
Best Practices by Industry

The kind of hiring processes you design and implement are heavily dependent on the industry you're in. Steps necessary for those looking to hire in the finance sector will be different from those required to hire in the medical sector, for example. For this reason, I think it's important to break down requirements by industry.

Again, these checklists are by no means exhaustive, and are no substitute for legal advice, given that state laws vary widely. However, they do make a good starting point. Below, I've outlined the recommended solutions for each of seven industry sectors. It should be possible to extrapolate a new checklist for related industries using this information as well. Customized solutions for your organization are always recommended as a preferred method to ensure the highest level of due diligence is exhausted.

The Finance/Banking Sector

Those working in the finance and banking sector rather obviously make security a high priority. Assuming that candidates will have possible access not only to liquid funds, but also to sensitive financial information means that background checks are generally among the most stringent that the law allows. For hiring in this sector, we recommend the following screenings:

- Social security and address history search verifying social security numbers and revealing not only past addresses but also potential aliases or other names associated with a number

- Statewide criminal history search where available (not in all states)

- Federal criminal history search

- DMV search to flag any potential criminal driving issues or behaviors including license suspensions

- E-Verify search to address whether a candidate is legally able to work in the U.S.

- Bankruptcy/liens/judgment search where legal to verify a candidate's financial position

- County civil search to find any civil actions

- Federal civil search to find any federal civil actions

- Credit report where legal to verify a candidate's financial position

- Employment verification to check a candidate's past job history

- Education verification to check a candidate's education and qualifications

- Reference follow-up for both professional and personal references listed

- Professional license verification where appropriate to check a candidate's professional qualifications

- Media search to check for any mention of a candidate in local/national/online media (must be done in accordance with FCRA guidelines)

- CBSV search to verify a candidate's social security number was issued by the U.S. government and is valid

- Social media search to identify any potential red flags in alignment with the FCRA

The Technology Sector

Working in the technology sector often requires that employees have access to sensitive and proprietary information including passwords, server identities, and programming code. For the tech sector we recommend the following kinds of screening:

- Social security and address history search verifying social security numbers and revealing not only past addresses but also potential aliases or other names associated with a number

- Statewide criminal history search where legal and available (not in all states)

- Federal criminal history search

- National sex offender registry search where applicable and legal

- National criminal search, which allows checking of crimes in multiple jurisdictions

- DMV search to flag any potential criminal driving issues or behaviors including license suspensions

- OFAC search, which involves checking with the Office of Foreign Assets Control to ensure that a candidate has not worked with agencies involved in terrorism, narcotics, or other disreputable activities

- Extended global sanctions search (GSA), which identifies candidates forbidden from working for the government, subcontracting for the government, or receiving certain governmental benefits or financial assistance

- E-Verify search to address whether a candidate is legally able to work in the U.S.

- Drug testing where appropriate and legal

- Compliance sanction search, which includes searching of things such as the FBI most wanted list, the Interpol most wanted list, and more

- Employment verification to check a candidate's past job history

- Education verification to check a candidate's education and qualifications

- Social media search to identify any potential red flags in alignment with the FCRA

The Energy Sector

Employment in the energy sector often requires candidates to have the knowledge and ability to operate sensitive and expensive equipment, as well as potential access to sensitive information and even financial records, and the ability to abide by governmental safety requirements including NERC best practices. For those hiring in the energy sector we recommend the following screenings:

- Social security and address history search verifying social security numbers and revealing not only past addresses but also potential aliases or other names associated with a number

- Statewide criminal history search where legal and available (not in all states)

- Federal criminal history search

- National sex offender registry search where applicable and legal

- National criminal search, which allows checking of crimes in multiple jurisdictions

- DMV search to flag any potential criminal driving issues

- OFAC search, which involves checking with the Office of Foreign Assets Control to ensure that a candidate has not worked with agencies involved in terrorism, narcotics, or other disreputable activities

- Extended global sanctions search (GSA), which identifies candidates forbidden from working for the government, subcontracting for the government, or receiving certain governmental benefits or financial assistance

- E-Verify search to address whether a candidate is legally able to work in the U.S.

- Drug testing where appropriate and legal

- Compliance sanction search, which includes searching of things such as the FBI most wanted list, the Interpol most wanted list, and more

The Gaming and Hospitality Sector

Working in the gaming and hospitality sector can obviously mean a candidate will have access to cash and financial details. However, successful candidates must also be able to provide a pleasant guest experience, or your company will face the prospect of visitors not returning. For those working in the gaming and hospitality sector we recommend the following:

- Social security and address history search verifying social security numbers and revealing not only past addresses but also potential aliases or other names associated with a number

- Statewide criminal history search where legal and available (not in all states)

- Federal criminal history search

- National sex offender registry search where applicable and legal

- National criminal search, which allows checking of crimes in multiple jurisdictions
- DMV search to flag any potential criminal driving issues or behaviors including license suspensions
- Bankruptcy/liens/judgment search where legal to verify a candidate's financial position
- Employment verification to check a candidate's past job history
- Professional reference verification to check a candidate's references from prior positions
- CBSV search to verify a candidate's social security number was issued by the U.S. government and is valid
- Social media search to identify any potential red flags in alignment with the FCRA
- Gaming Commission license verification status

The Transportation Sector

In the transportation sector candidates can be exposed to any number of assets and any amount of personal information. A clean driving record and responsible driving history are a must, and there may also be additional state laws that you must abide by when hiring. For the transportation sector we recommend the following screenings:

- Social security and address history search verifying social security numbers and revealing not only past addresses but also potential aliases or other names associated with a number
- Statewide criminal history search where legal and available (not in all states)
- Federal criminal history search

- National criminal search, which allows checking of crimes in multiple jurisdictions

- DMV search to flag any potential criminal driving issues

- OFAC search, which involves checking with the Office of Foreign Assets Control to ensure that a candidate has not worked with agencies involved in terrorism, narcotics, or other disreputable activities

- E-Verify search to address whether a candidate is legally able to work in the U.S.

- Drug testing where appropriate and legal

- The DMV LENS program (in New York, for example; other programs may apply in other states), which constantly reviews DMV records and reports current infractions during working days. This information includes reports about accidents, hazardous material endorsements, medical certification changes, suspensions and revocations, expirations, convictions, and point and insurance reduction program changes.

- Existence of CDL's in other regions/states

- Employment verification to check a candidate's past job history

- DOT employment verifications, which will show prior job performance as well as information about accidents, drug or alcohol performance issues, and the like while the candidate was on the job

- FMCSA status and verification

The Staffing Sector

Working in the staffing sector can mean that employees have access to a myriad of different kinds of information, equipment, and data. And in temporary staffing solutions, the kind of access an employee has may be constantly changing. This could mean you need to run all of the following kinds of screening. However, if your company works on staffing with only certain kinds of other industries, you may be able to eliminate some of the below checks. The array of screenings we recommend that those in the staffing sector consider are:

- Social security and address history search verifying social security numbers and revealing not only past addresses but also potential aliases or other names associated with a number

- Statewide criminal history search where legal and available (not in all states)

- Federal criminal history search

- National sex offender registry search where applicable and legal

- National criminal search, which allows checking of crimes in multiple jurisdictions

- DMV search to flag any potential criminal driving issues

- Employment verification to check a candidate's past job history

- Education verification to check a candidate's education and qualifications

- Professional license verification where appropriate to check a candidate's professional qualifications

- E-Verify search to address whether a candidate is legally able to work in the U.S.

- Drug testing where appropriate and legal

The Healthcare Sector

Finally, the healthcare sector is one that is particularly sensitive, given the amount of personal data and even financial information candidates may have access to. And obviously, appropriate professional credentials and qualifications will be necessary. Due to high risk of malpractice and theft, candidates for all medical sector jobs must be thoroughly vetted. For the healthcare industry we recommend the following checks:

- Social security and address history search verifying social security numbers and revealing not only past addresses but also potential aliases or other names associated with a number
- Statewide criminal history search where legal and available (not in all states)
- Federal criminal history search
- National sex offender registry search where applicable and legal
- National criminal search, which allows checking of crimes in multiple jurisdictions
- DMV search to flag any potential criminal driving issues
- OFAC search, which involves checking with the Office of Foreign Assets Control to ensure that a candidate has not worked with agencies involved in terrorism, narcotics, or other disreputable activities
- Extended global sanctions search (GSA), which identifies candidates forbidden from working for the government, subcontracting for the government, or receiving certain governmental benefits or financial assistance
- E-Verify search to address whether a candidate is legally able to work in the U.S.
- Drug testing where appropriate and legal

- Office of the inspector general (OIG) search, which shows candidates excluded from federally funded healthcare programs such as Medicare and Medicaid

- Office of the Medicaid inspector general search, which shows those who are excluded from working with Medicaid due to unethical behavior

- CBSV search to verify a candidate's social security number

- Healthcare compliance search, which includes those debarred and blocked from various sources such as the Department of Health Services Debarment List, the OIG Health & Human Services Exclusion List, Adult Abuse lists, and the FDA Debarment List

- Employment verification to check a candidate's past job history

- Education verification to check a candidate's education and qualifications

- Professional license verification where appropriate to check a candidate's professional qualifications

- Professional license monitoring to continually ensure that a candidate's license to practice is up to date

- Professional reference verification to check a candidate's references from prior positions

- Healthcare sanction monitoring to continually monitor the healthcare sanction database and ensure that a candidate has not been sanctioned

Again, these checklists are not exhaustive. There may be other screenings that you decide are necessary, and there may be included screenings that you feel are unnecessary or that violate laws in your location. However, they do provide a solid starting point. If you're serious about hiring the right candidates and mitigating your risks as an organization, these are all checks that you'll need to consider.

Chapter Twelve

Summary and Closing

Throughout this book I have done my utmost to convince you that an applicant's past can be your future if proper risk mitigation in the form of due diligence is not done. It is critical that you have well rounded, legally compliant processes to conduct proper investigations on all employees, contractors, and gig workers. And not only during the hiring period! Ongoing screening during the course of an applicant's employment is also key.

The risk to you as an organization presented by employing the wrong candidate is more than just financial. You risk your reputation, your time, and your effort alongside your assets both financial and otherwise. The costs of the wrong hire can be immense.

Your work begins with the initial hiring process. How do you find your target candidates? How do you ensure that they are a good fit for your company? How can you screen candidates to make sure that they are not presenting risk to you and your organization? And most of all, how do you ensure that you are following legal requirements in your hiring process?

This is all complicated by the fact that the nature of candidates and hiring is changing. Gig workers and contractors are becoming more and more popular, and they represent different challenges when it comes to hiring, screening, and onboarding.

And once you have made the decision to hire, you must then move on to ensuring a solid onboarding process, as well as thinking about continuing screening. I have made this point many times in this book, but I'd like to make it one last time: Life happens. Circumstances change, people change, and just because a candidate was found suitable during his initial screening does not mean he or she will continue to be suitable. Infinity screening is the only way to stay up to date with the changes in an employee's situation.

We have touched on the vast amount of legal obligations that must be taken into account when hiring and firing. This is a rapidly changing set of guidelines that must be adhered to if you wish to avoid potential future problems. Laws vary by state, and what is necessary in one location may not be necessary in another, and vice versa.

The best way to mitigate risk in hiring and employment is to have set internal procedures that are followed with each candidate and employee, taking into account best practices when dealing with both employees and contractors or gig workers. These procedures and practices should help ensure that your HR department performs efficiently and that you stay on the right side of the law while still keeping your risk level low.

Finally, we discussed the continuing challenges that are presented post-hire, where instituting processes to deal with situations such as disciplinary issues or poor job performance or even the surprises thrown up by a standard regular screening will help again mitigate your risks. And of course, we discussed avoiding litigation, because no one wants to be sued.

My aim for this book is that you are now in a position to make better, more compliant, less risky decisions when hiring and keeping workers. Your organization is important—why take risks that are unnecessary?

Allowing a worker to enter your organization is like inviting a stranger into your living room. Without knowing that person, you have no idea what consequences your offer or invitation can have. However, with the appropriate due diligence you can mitigate your risks. An applicant's past can be your future – but it doesn't have to be. If you follow the procedures in this book, you will be equipped with best practices for avoiding costly hiring mistakes!

www.allianceinvestigative.com

Facebook:
facebook.com/Alliance-Worldwide-Investigative-Group-Inc-339133645709/

Linkedin:
linkedin.com/company/alliance-worldwide-investigative-group-inc-

Twitter:
twitter.com/AWIGINC

About the Author

Mario S. Pecoraro is an entrepreneur, corporate visionary, and founder of Alliance Worldwide Investigative Group, which specializes in background screening, insurance fraud investigations, and risk mitigation. He graduated from the University of New York at Albany with degrees in criminal justice and Italian. He lives with his wife JoJo in Clifton Park, New York.